Sheila Leeds

Martin Zender is known as The World's Most Outspoken Bible Scholar. He is an essayist, conference speaker, radio personality, humorist, and the author of several books on spiritual freedom. His essays have appeared in the *Chicago Tribune*, the *Atlanta Journal-Constitution*, the *Cleveland Plain Dealer*, and other newspapers. He has hosted the Grace Café radio program at WCCD in Cleveland, and the syndicated Zender/Sheridan Show at flagship station WBRI in Indianapolis.

www.martinzender.com

Divine Principles of Sexual Attraction

July 9, 2020

To my friend Sarah,

Grace + Peace —

[illegible]

Also by Martin Zender

Eve Raised

Beyond Politics

Flawed by Design

How to Quit Church
Without Quitting God

The First Idiot in Heaven

Martin Zender's Guide
to Intelligent Prayer

How To Be Free From Sin
While Smoking a Cigarette

Martin Zender Goes To Hell

The Really Bad Thing About Free Will

Clanging Gong News: The Complete Issues

Divine Principles of Sexual Attraction

How women are like God
and why men want to worship them

Starke & Hartmann, Inc.

Divine Principles of Sexual Attraction

Published by Starke & Hartmann
P.O. Box 6473
Canton, OH 44706
www.starkehartmann.com
1-866-866-BOOK

Printed in the United States of America

Publisher's Cataloging-In-Publication Data
(Prepared by The Donohue Group, Inc.)

Names: Zender, Martin.
Title: Divine principles of sexual attraction : [how women are like God and why men want to worship them] / Martin Zender.
Description: Canton, OH : Starke & Hartmann, [2018]
Identifiers: ISBN 9780984254859 | ISBN 0984254854 | ISBN 9780984254866 (ebook) | ISBN 0984254862 (ebook)
Subjects: LCSH: Sex--Religious aspects--Christianity. | Man-woman relationships--Religious aspects--Christianity. | Sexual attraction. | Women--Religious aspects--Christianity.
Classification: LCC BT708 .Z46 2018 (print) | LCC BT708 (ebook) | DDC 241.66--dc23

Photo credits: The following photos © Can Stock Photo: Cover photo and pg. 7: songbird839; pg. 17: andersonrise; pg. 25: Fotosmurf; pg. 31: stokkete; pg. 62: dolgachov; pg. 73:ggprophoto; pg. 79: showface; pg. 82: JackF; pg. 87: aletia; pg. 89: leafy; pg. 92:gtoh; pg. 97: dachazworks; pg. 100: coka; pg. 103: avesun; pg. 109: Scented mirror; pg. 117: konradbak.

The following photos: flickr.com, attribution only (https://creativecommons.org/licenses/by/2.0/): pg. 32: Timothy Krause; pg. 40: Zabara Alexander; pg. 43: David Martyn Hunt; pg. 57: 1950sUnlimited; pg. 53: Gustav Vigeland; pg. 113: jin.Dongjun.

Pg. 50, Lennon and Ono: © Annie Leibovitz

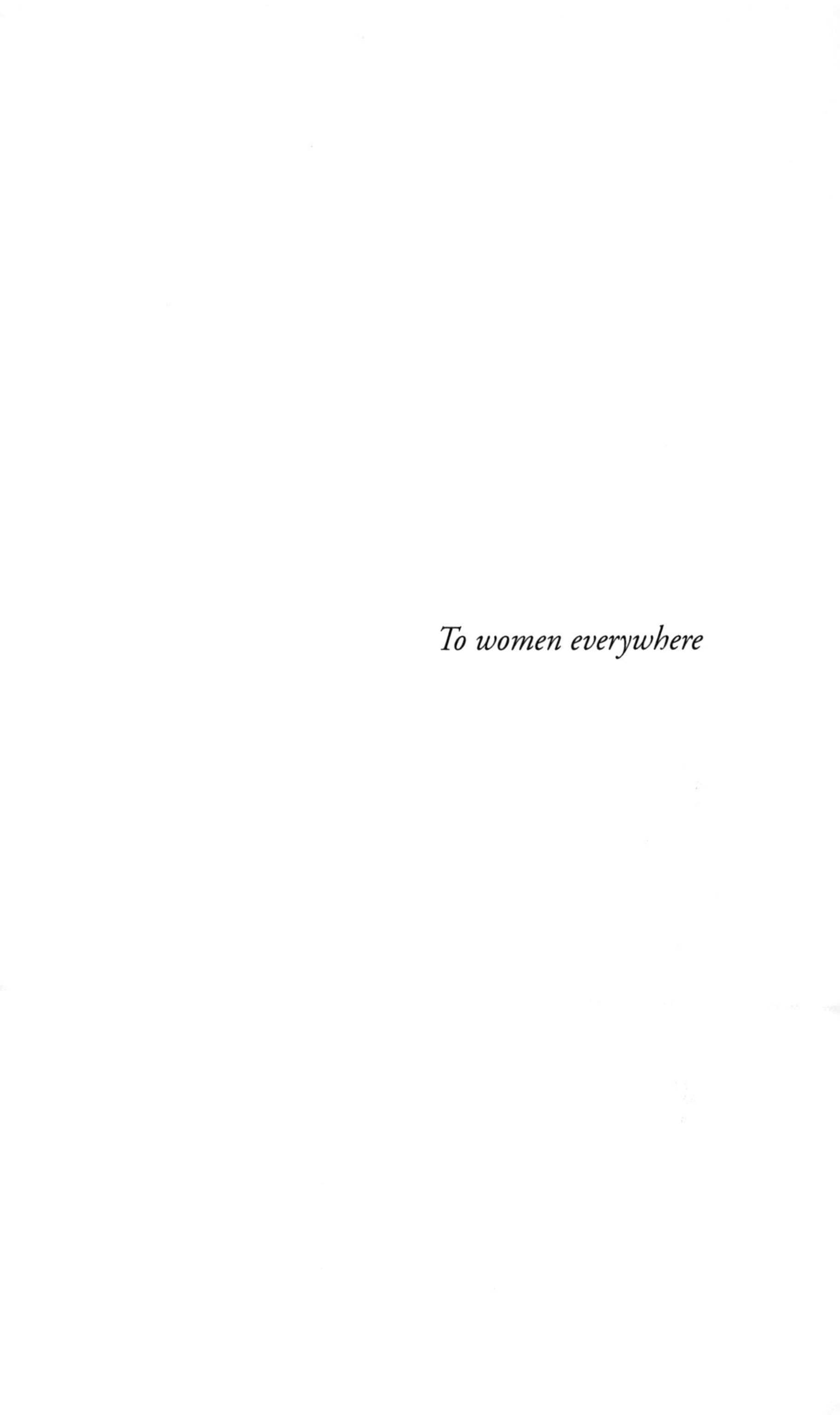

To women everywhere

"As a deer is panting over the channels of water, so is my soul panting for You, O Elohim."

—Psalm 42:1

The parable of woman

God's universe is full of parables. The sun, for example, appears to rise and set. The Creator could have made Earth stationary (you'd think it would have been easier for Him, what with inertia and all), but instead He licked His finger and sent us spinning around an axis. We face the sun and then don't face it, over and over again. Why? It's a parable illustrating the most glorious truth in God's universe, namely, that light dispels darkness, and not the other way around. This is God's divine order; darkness first, then light. This is why the Jewish day begins at sundown rather than sunup. Darkness and light themselves, however, are metaphors of the greater truths of evil and good. Night after night, day after day, 365 days a year, this celestial picture book that we call dawn testifies to the grand goal of God: Good (light) will one day overcome evil (darkness), for all time. As the Scriptures testify:

> The heavens are recounting the glory of God, and the atmosphere is telling the work of His hands. Day after day is uttering a saying, and night after night is disclosing knowledge. There is no audible saying, and there are no words; their voice is unheard. Yet into the entire earth their voice goes forth, and into the ends of the habitance their declarations.
> —*Psalm 19:1-4*

What about the seasons? God not only spins the earth, He hurls it around the sun in an elliptical orbit at 67,000 miles per hour, angling it, simultaneously, at twenty-three degrees. Why the warped path? How come the crazy pitch? Moderation is a terrible teacher. We are sent here to know extremes: cold, heat, death, life, dread, and comfort. An upright, immobile planet gives us none of these; it's why God sent the planet sailing and spinning long before we moved in. Look outside and learn the lesson: from December through March, God kills; from April through May, He makes alive. Do you get it? Do you hear the voiceless language? It's another parable, picturing for us the great truth that resurrection succeeds death. Out goes this voice, year after year, winter after freezing winter. Throughout the span of this parable's existence, spring has never once failed to say: *Life will one day displace, forever, our most dreaded enemy: death.*

In another part of the universe, a long-legged young woman in a short, flouncy skirt walks from Bryant Street to Washington Avenue. This is occurring in the sector of God's creation known as Dallas, Texas. Sheila is eating lunch today

at Exall Park, and has to hurry there. Through no fault of her own, her hips roll when she walks fast. Why did it have to be so warm today? She evaporates moisture through a sleeveless, gauzy blouse, fitted at the sides with ingenious little tucks. Her haunches—in rhythm with her long auburn ponytail—swing from side to side with each purposely-placed heel of her tall, black boots.

Twelve men at a construction site on Bryant Street stop to watch her. They were working on a multimillion-dollar office building—note the word "were." As long as Sheila walks, this building will sit dead on its footers. It will not go up, ever.

"God!" says one of the men.

Interesting. He instinctively knows the parable.

Another man, Ed, is more talkative than the man who related Sheila to the Deity.

"I would lie down naked on Washington Avenue in freezing weather so that this woman could cross the street on my back," he exclaims with a strange calm. (Don't shoot the messenger. I overheard this—for real. I am but a social commentator. Though I don't make these things up, I do explain them.) The other men nod.

Why would anyone say something like that? It's so unbalanced. It's so elliptical. It's so tilted at a twenty-three-degree angle.

The magnetism between men and women is the most powerful, most prolific force on Earth. It is a power that launches armies, shatters kingdoms, and destroys as many lives as it generates. Why is it so ridiculously—*strong?*

Many would say: procreation. Yet God could certainly bring more human beings into the world without, say, spaghetti straps. Or Brut cologne. Or kissing; why the urge to mesh mouths in the first place? What does the exchange of saliva have to do with the transference of seed? And this: does the race perish apart from red roses? Lace-topped stockings? Satin sheets? I am wondering now about soft music and candlelight. Can we not duplicate ourselves without Ravel's *Boléro?*

I just read a strange sentence on the Internet a few moments ago in an article titled, "Sex After Sixty." A woman whom I will call Mrs. Henderson said: "I did not have my first orgasm until age eighty-four." How can a sentence like this even exist? Is it safe to say that something besides procreation may be occurring here?

Many things less significant than sex and the sun picture divine truth. Jesus set forth lilies and sparrows as parables of God's care. Additionally, when we see a lamb we're to think of Jesus Christ's meekness (He called Himself, "the Lamb of God"), while the lion calls to mind His strength ("the Lion of Judah").

The apostle Paul picks up a kernel of wheat and says, *Do you people want to know truth?*

Sure, Paul.

Then study a kernel of wheat.

What do you mean?

The apostle holds up the small kernel he has just unearthed. "What you are sowing is not being vivified if it should not be dying" (1 Corinthians 15:36). He shakes his head in utter amazement and then shoves the kernel back into the soil with his big thumb.

If a seed, a lily, a small bird and a lamb picture such monumental truths, what of this power that, second-by-second, rattles the globe? If procreation is this power's fundamental *raison d'etre,* then why is eighty-four-year-old Mrs. Henderson, bless her heart, only now tapping its potency four decades past her childbearing prime?

God could have caused babies to spring up from the ground like corn, or sent them to petitioning humans via the stork. For that matter, He could have made sex clinical: 1) enter procreation booth, 2) draw curtain, 3) insert bolt A into locknut B, 4) wait nine months, and 5) withdraw baby. But no. As with the universe-at-large, moderation is a terrible teacher. God doesn't want it calm and clean. We are sent here to know extremes: desire, denial, longing, and fulfillment. In short, we are sent to find God.

This may explain corsets.

Sexual passion is a parable so high that it dwarfs even the sun and stars in the realm of revelation: *Sexual power pictures for us the drawing power of God. The power of a woman to draw a man is a microcosm of God's ability and intention to return all humanity to Himself.*

The source of sexual power

It was Adam, not Eve, from whom God withdrew a vital part. Thus, Adam awoke from the world's first surgical procedure with a lack unknown to his wife. This lack turned into a longing, and the longing is what pushed him toward her. Note: it is what pushed *him* toward *her; he* took the first step, not the woman. Contrary to the common translations, God did not remove a rib from Adam to build Eve. "Rib" is in no way suggested by the original Hebrew text. (The very concept is absurd.) The word for an anatomical rib is *ala,* but the word here in this context is *tsela.* It was, in fact, the uterus that Adam lost—the female sex organ. (More on this in the next chapter.)

Prior to Eve's creation, Adam was a complete human being containing both sexes. Today, this is an anomaly but not *that* uncommon, and we call people who are born with both sexual organs "hermaphrodites." Such an anomaly belongs to the human genetic code because the first human was exactly this. God separated the sexes in Eden.

The details of this truth will astound you; the specifics of Adam's lack ring true not only Scripturally and anatomically, but socially. Men act as they do because of this lack, and women likewise because of their lack of the lack. Thus, Eden becomes the inaugural demonstration of sexual *power* and the new movement (man toward woman) belonging to it. Remember? God doesn't like things standing still. With everything he needed inside of him, Adam stood still. With his female essence removed, however, motion began—for now the female was outside of him. What does a man long for in the marriage embrace? Certainly not his missing rib. In the human sexual power dynamic, it is the female who entices and draws, not the male. Because his emptiness exceeded hers (nothing was removed from Eve), Adam fell toward his wife, and not vice-versa. This motion began in Eden and hasn't stopped yet—

> Therefore a man shall forsake his father and his mother and cling to his wife.
>
> —*Genesis 2:24*

It is the man who is instructed to cling, not the wife. Nowhere in Scripture are wives instructed to cling to their husbands. Genesis 2:24 is less instruction to the man than it is a statement of fact concerning him. In other words: this is what the man *shall* do—watch him.

The word "cling" smacks of desperation and compulsion, as well it should.

The Hebrew word translated "cling" in the Concordant Version of the Old Testament is *dabaq*. Notably, some passages in Deuteronomy apply this word to God—

> Yahweh your Elohim shall you fear, and Him shall you serve; to Him shall you cling (*dabaq*), and by His Name shall you swear. He is your praise, and He is your Elohim Who did for you these great and fear-inspiring deeds that your eyes saw. Hence you will love Yahweh your Elohim and observe His charge, His statutes, His ordinances and His instructions all the days (10:20, 22; 11:1).

No one can cling physically to God. How we wish we could. At least the apostle John could recline on Jesus' chest (John 13:23) at the Last Supper. I would drop to my knees and hug Jesus—if I could. How wonderful that would feel. We forget that worship, in the next life, will be an exercise of body as well as of heart and spirit. After all, we will possess bodies in the resurrection (1 Corinthians 15:44). We will not be wisps. We will still have emotions. We will still desire physical proximity to other beings—and God will not disappoint.

Jesus Christ has a body. The present, physical absence of our Lord is temporarily and partly cured by marriage. Here's what I mean: God was present with Adam from the beginning. Adam walked and talked with God in the Garden of Eden. (As God is absolutely invisible, the fellowship was presumably conducted between Adam and God's designated Image—Colossians 1:15—that is, the pre-Bethlehem Christ.) When Eve came along, it was somewhat like Yoko Ono entering the Beatles' circle. After Yoko came, John was distracted. Before that, it was John, Paul, and the other guys. Now it was John hanging mostly with Yoko. A separation had come. Back to the Garden of Eden, and God wanted Adam tending to Eve now. Eve was God's Yoko Ono—though willingly served into the scene and accepted. That's why God said that Adam was to cling to his wife. To whom did he cling before that? Not to the kangaroo. He clung to God, that is, to His designated Image. Thus, Eve becomes, for Adam, a proxy-God. She becomes God's own substitute for Himself. He goes away, and she enters. Not coincidentally, marriage is abolished when the kingdom arrives. Of course. With God's Image reintroduced physically into the world, the temporary respite and parable of the sexes is necessarily abolished, its purpose having been served.

The clinging of Deuteronomy 10:20, just mentioned, is metaphoric. The sense there is that Israel was to cling to God with her heart and mind. Yet the metaphor is based on literal clinging; Adam was to literally cling to his wife. Here is an example of literal and metaphoric clinging in the same verse—

> For just as the belt clings to a man's waist, so I have caused all the house of Israel and all the house of Judah to cling to Me, saying is Yahweh, to become Mine, for a people and for a name, and for praise and for beauty.
>
> —*Jeremiah 13:11*

I love clinging to my wife's waist. The best posture, for me, is on my knees with my arms wrapped around her hips, the side of my face pressed against her stomach. I will repeatedly kiss her hips and stomach. My wife is a beautifully-crafted woman. I kiss my wife's hips in the same manner Gomez Addams used to kiss his wife Morticia's

right arm whenever she spoke French. My wife's flared hips and narrow waist provide, for me, a shelter from the storm of this hard world. Clinging to her, I am transported—if only for a moment—into the throne room of God's love and grace. I can't kiss Him, but I can kiss the hell out of her, and I do.

In the physical absence of Deity, this satisfies. In the clinging scenario, my wife gains equal good; receiving my adoration and love is her part of the divine parable of the sexes which, again, illustrates the drawing power of God upon humanity and humanity's innate need to worship Him. In other words, receiving does for my wife what clinging does for me; it shelters her from the storm. She likes to hug me but has no bend for the kind of clinging that I instinctively engage in. It is simply not in her to do it; God did not wire her that way. Dog-like fawning and clinging is the male end of the parable. I cling, my wife gets clung to, and we each enjoy our respective roles. It's symbiotic perfection. Until Jesus returns, this does fine. Yes, and God has meant for it to do fine. We ought to take advantage of it—all of us—up until the day it is abolished. The return of Christ triggers its abolition.

This flowing of the sexual power from Adam toward Eve coincides with the first pair's respective anatomies: Adam's anatomy goes outward, toward Eve, while Eve's organ of reception slopes inward, toward herself. All goes toward the woman. It's perfectly illustrative. These physiological motions (and non-motions) underlie and define sexual attraction; no, they *are* sexual attraction. The "outward" and "inward" of the respective anatomical components constitute physical evidence of the direction (man toward woman) of the invisible power/sex flow.

> Therefore a man shall forsake his father and his mother and cling to his wife.
>
> —*Genesis 2:24*

> And I, if I should be exalted out of the earth, shall be drawing all to Myself.
>
> —*John 12:32*

> As a deer is panting over the channels of water, so is my soul panting for You, O Elohim.
>
> —*Psalm 42:1*

Clinging, drawing, panting. Such drastic verbs. Should we apply them to God or to the sexes? Both. *Sexual power pictures for us the drawing power of God.* In the spiritual realm, it is God Who draws; humanity moves toward and clings to Him. In the sexual realm, woman draws; man moves toward and clings to her. Thus, in the parable, the woman represents God, while the man represents humanity as a whole.

Adam's name, *Adm,* means, "of the ground." Eve's Hebrew name, *Chavvah*, means, "life," or, more literally, "life-spring." All human life springs from her, making her more like the Deity than Adam. Eve emerged from Adam, yes, but Adam no more consciously produced her than a tree consciously produces a chair; the man was snoring at the time of the procedure. In contrast to this, Eve *does* produce life, and expels it consciously from the core of her being. In this, she is God-like.

The female is the giver of human life. She is also the sun of the sexual universe. Human life begins with sex, which itself begins with the drawing power of a woman. Conversely, God is the center of the universe; He gives to all, all (Acts 17:25). Spiritual life begins with God, Who Himself initiates this by His own inherent power to draw humanity to Himself.

I am comparing women to God—in case you haven't noticed. This is God's parable, and it is holy.

Tsela

In the beginning, *Elohim* created the *shamayim* and *erets* (heavens and earth), made a few fish, animals and birds, then raised an even more startling creature from the dust of the ground, calling it *Adm* (that's the original Hebrew word for "Adam"). Elohim settled Adm into a garden called *Odn*. Just when the angels imagined that Elohim had outdone Himself, He put Adm to sleep and pulled from him an even more startling creature: *Ishshah*. Elohim was so pleased with *this* creation, and the effect of Ishshah upon the collective breath of the celestial world, that He has refused to make anything since.

I'm traveling back in time to the source of sexual power. I'm using the Hebrew words to freshen our perspective. *Elohim* is the Hebrew word for God (it means "Subjector"), *shamayim* is heaven, *erets* is earth. The Garden of Eden is *Odn* in the ancient texts, and the first human was called *Adm*, which means "of the ground." But the Hebrew word for man (the male human) is *ish*, which I'm turning into a personal pronoun. As for the creature that stunned the universe, her formal name was *Chavvah* (English makes this "Eve," or "life"), but I am calling her *Ishshah* (the Hebrew equivalent of "woman"), because it is a very sexy collection of consonants and vowels.

People make fun of the Bible because they think it contains ridiculous accounts that could not possibly have happened—things like Noah's ark and Adam and Eve. These things seem just too unlikely and ridiculous to the advanced brains of modern "thinkers." What people generally don't realize is that God does ridiculous things on purpose. He's not trying to look smart and failing. He's not trying to impress humanity with feats of great genius and falling pitiably short. God is out to prove that His foolishness is wiser than the wisdom of humans (1 Corinthians 1:25), and I suspect that He's doing it. After all is said and done, the world will realize that, compared to Einstein's Theory of Relativity, Noah's ark was brilliance afloat.

We are not yet equipped to see God's wisdom.

But in some places, the Bible is stranger than it needs to be. This is due to poor translating. Take the creation of Adm, for instance. It's strange enough learning that Elohim formed Adm from the soil. We can almost believe it, however, as science has since proven that we're organic; all the elements of our bodies are traceable to the soil. But next we are informed that Elohim put Adm to sleep, removed one of his ribs, and built from it a woman. Now we're rolling our eyes. Some are even laughing out loud. The following is taken from the King James Version, Genesis 2:21-22—

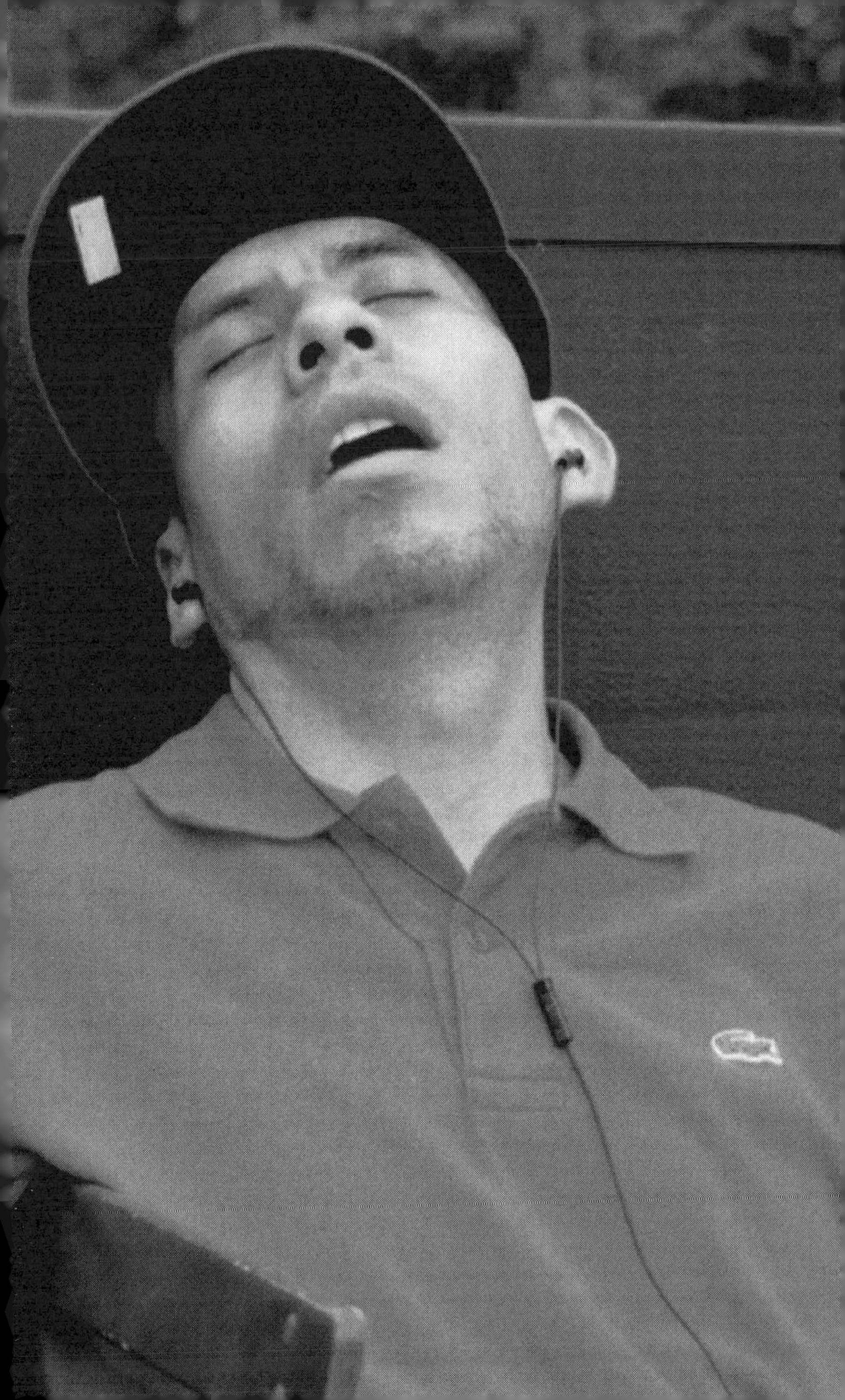

> And the Lord God caused a deep sleep to fall upon Adam, and he slept: and He took one of his ribs, and closed up the flesh instead thereof; and the rib, which the Lord God had taken from man, made He a woman, and brought her unto the man.

Even though the idea of building woman from a rib seems absurd, Christian-types believe it because it's "in the Bible." Noah is starting to look smarter already. At least we can grasp the concept of the ark account: a large boat rescues humans and animals from a worldwide flood. But a rib from which to build the first woman? The apparent absurdity and purposelessness of it strains even hardcore believers.

The thing is, it wasn't a rib. Elohim did not take a rib from Adm to build Ishshah. He took something else.

If Elohim had taken a rib in preparation for His last great creative act, then in Genesis 2:21-22, where the event is described, we would see the Hebrew equivalent of the Chaldee *ala,* used in Daniel 7:5 to describe a proper, anatomical rib. But that word is not here. Instead, we find the Hebrew word *tsela,* which means "a hollow, angular vault." A hollow, angular vault? Yes. Bear with me; this is going to pay off.

This same word, *tsela,* appears repeatedly in Ezekiel 41:5-26 to describe the side rooms of the Israelite temple. From Ezekiel 41:6,7—

> And the side chambers (*tsela*) were in three stories, one above another, and thirty in each story...and the side chambers (*tsela*) surrounding the temple were wider at each successive story.

Study the illustration below. Though not strictly accurate or drawn to scale, this is the general idea. The walls of the temple were hollow and contained rooms. These were by no means ribs, but hollow chambers, or vaults. A unique characteristic of the rooms is that they tapered from top to bottom, narrowing with each descending story. Anyone wishing to verify this can read 1 Kings 6:6. I'll save you the trouble—

> The lowest story was five cubits wide, and the middle was six cubits wide, and the third was seven cubits wide.

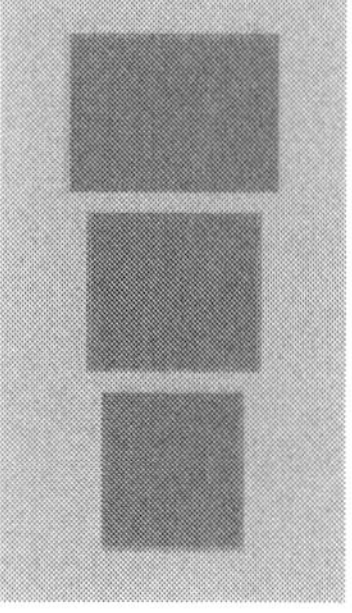

Tsela was not a rib? Then why did the King James translators, in the Genesis account, make it "rib"? Because they took *tsela* to be the location of the thing taken, rather than the shape. They saw *tsela* in Genesis and said, "What is this?" Someone said, "It's the same word used in Ezekiel to describe the side rooms of the temple." The word "side" got passed around, and the conclusion was, "This was something from Adam's side. It must have been a rib." But God did not mean this word to describe the location of what He took, but the shape. It was something shaped like the temple sidewalls, that is, hollow and angular, tapering from top to bottom.

The structure you are now considering, below, is the human uterus, otherwise known as the womb. It is an angular, hollow chamber, tapering from top to bottom, the exclusive property of Ishshah. Is it possible that this is the thing Elohim removed from Adm, to build Ishshah? No; it *is* the thing Elohim removed from Adm to build Ishshah.

Here is Genesis 2:21-22 from the *Concordant Version of the Old Testament*, a very accurate and consistent rendering of the Hebrew—

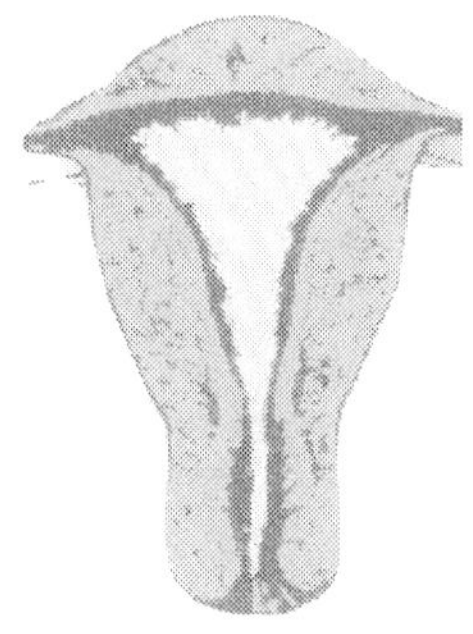

> And falling is a stupor on the human, caused by Yahweh Elohim, and he is sleeping. And taking is He one of his *angular organs* and is closing the flesh under it. And Yahweh Elohim is building the angular organ, which He takes from the human, into a woman.

This explains everything.

Six Inches Into The Kingdom

At one time, Adam was complete in himself. He contained both sexes. In short, he had it all. He had all the grace, sensitivity, and silken beauty that the woman would possess, as well as the strength and ruggedness that we associate with masculinity.

It wasn't that Eve was absent, but that she was inherent in Adam, which was originally the name of the race. Adam was neither male nor female, but both. He became male only upon the removal of the woman from him. Here in Eden there stood, for a brief period in history prior to the separation, the perfect human being.

Yet something was missing. Two things, really: longing and appreciation.

Adam wanted for nothing. He had no need. He walked and talked with God all day, enjoying an unbroken spiritual connection with Him. Physically, he nourished himself with the plentiful fruits of Eden, and he did so without struggle. Yet search the Genesis account, and you will not find one word of praise from the lips of Adam, not one "thank you" for any of these blessings. How could this be?

With no sense of longing, there can be no sense of appreciation.

Adam must have imagined that it would go on like this forever. But God had something better in mind. It was in His mind, always, to create beings in which He could implant a sense of deep need and thus deep satisfaction upon the fulfillment of the need. Was Adam satisfied in Eden? He would not even have understood the concept. "Satisfaction" is an impossible sensation for a being knowing nothing but satiation; there is no contrast. So where does longing come from in a universe void of it? Where longing does not yet exist, it must be created.

"And falling is a stupor on the human, caused by Yahweh God, and he is sleeping."

With Adam now asleep upon the very ground of his making, God prepares to divide the race and create the most powerful and desperate sensation of longing on the face of the earth—

> And taking is He one of his angular organs and is closing the flesh under it. And Yahweh God is building the angular organ, which He takes from the human, into a woman.

For "angular organ" (here in the *Concordant Version of the Old Testament*), the *Dabhar Version* (another consistent translation) has "cell." This is cell not in the biological sense, but in the sense of what a prisoner sits in. I prefer "chamber" to both "angular organ" and "cell" because of the Ezekiel contexts of *tsela,* where the word describes rooms. The *Concordant Version* is good in that it suggests the shape of the thing that God took. God removed "one of" Adam's chambers, suggesting that he has others, which he has—speaking of his organs.

So now Adam lacked some vital chamber (organ) that the new creature (Eve) now possessed.

I want you to watch carefully what happens next, because it is the genesis of what has happened ever since—in bars, brothels, classrooms, bedrooms, ballrooms, parking lots, movie theaters and the street—wherever men and women feel the first pull of power.

Adam opens his eyes. He blinks to find that he is staring at the sky. *Why am I flat on my back?* he wonders. *Where am I, and how did I get here?* His sense of hearing returns, and the rushing of water becomes so dominant that he ignores an odd tingling at the tips of his fingers. When he does note the tingling, he is amazed at how it moves from his fingertips, up his arms, across his chest, then down the length of his body. It does not hurt, but neither does he like it. He wants it to stop.

He realizes now from the strong sound of water that he is lying near the river Gihon. Things are starting to come back to him. He had been taking a walk. He must have lain down to sleep, but he never sleeps near any of the rivers. He sleeps in the south of Eden, always, by the quartz fields. He remembers, maybe, sitting down to rest. After that, nothing.

A strong wind blows dirt across his face and he turns his head to the left to avoid the wind. The trees are bending to the weight of the wind. He has never seen trees behave like this. There has never been this much wind. He is fascinated

by the wind and the bending of the trees. He looks at this through blinking eyes for what seems to him like a long time, then rolls his head back to center. He closes his eyes again.

He is aware now of his breathing; he is conscious of his naked chest heaving up and down through the different air. He concentrates on the heaving. All the tingling has left his body, but there is a heaviness inside of him that he has never felt. He describes it to himself as a weight, though it has nothing to do with weight, but with lack. His own explanation makes no sense to him, so he abandons it. Something very strange has happened to him—he knows this much—and he pulls his knees toward his chest. He must get up.

Rolling over onto his left side, the first human being steadies himself on an elbow. *Why is this so difficult?* He rights himself with his left arm and is sitting now. A long wet lock of hair drops over his eyes; he pushes it away. As soon as he pushes away the lock, he feels stronger. He drags his hand now, with parted fingers, over and over through his black hair, pushing it backward over his head. Strength is returning to him.

He struggles to his feet and stands upright. He cannot balance, then suddenly he can, but then once again he cannot. Something is definitely not right. He is staring at the trees now, and noticing that the wind has completely stopped.

His breath shortens, and his lips quiver involuntarily. One side of his mouth is turning up on its own, toward his nose. He grabs for it, panicked. His fingers are shaking uncontrollably. His eyes fill with water and he cannot see anything now except waving colors. A quaking sensation comes to his throat and he wonders if he will be able to draw another breath. *God! What is happening!*

"Adam. My *man*."

Adam turns almost ferociously to his right, toward the sound. With this violent motion, he has betrayed to the universe his first pang of fear. This was not the voice of God. Nothing yet comes into view. The world seems full of water vapor, and so he forms both hands into fists, trying to wipe it away from his eyes. His body trembles as he strains toward the sound, to detect it, to detect what made it.

"Adam. My *man*."

"I am Adam! What are you?"

The world clears. If the quaking in the throat of the formerly most perfect human rocked him before, the convulsion *this* time brings his hands toward the top of his head in a gesture of wondering if he has lost his mind. "I am Adam!" he says again, and a form—a being—appears gradually through the vapors.

And where before there was nothing against this same blue sky, there appears a creature now, much like himself, yet with eye-arresting differences. *What is this?* The fear that Adam felt is gone, and he stares hard at the differences of the new being. "I am Adam!" he says again, surprised at the coarseness of his own voice, yet still staring at the differences.

"I am Ishshah," says the strange new being, searching for meaning in the eyes of the first human.

Eve does not move toward Adam, and there is a profound reason for it: she feels no relief to see him. He is new, but so is everything else. Eve does not lack. Nothing has been taken from her. Her most immediate need, then, is to discover why she is here. Adam was also complete before God removed *tsela*. But he awoke from the procedure with an unknown ache. The feeling that he at first could not discern—what he

at first thought was weight—was emptiness.

Those first few minutes after looking at the trees, when he fought that first human urge to cry, felt to Adam like an hour. Eve had watched it all from the water's edge. Then she called the first man's name—the name whispered to her by God—and when Adam finally turned to see what had called him, it was his eyes that Eve sought, not his body, for she instinctively knew these to be the conduits of his intelligence.

Adam realized almost immediately that this was his relief, his answer, his completion, the filling of his new and terrible lack. And at the precise moment of this revelation—something happened. I'm struggling now with how to record it so as to lend it the singularity and profundity it possessed. I am aware that it was the first occurrence of what we now call human *eroticism*, but it was also the first parable of humanity, as a race, seeking something greater than itself—something above. Adam sensed it for certain, and he at last pulled his eyes from Eve to watch it. Something was happening with *talah.*

Talah is Hebrew for "hanging," and this is what I have chosen to call that part of Adam no longer hanging but rising—as though possessed by an independent life source—toward the woman. Eve could not help but take her eyes from Adam's eyes and look to see what was rising from his midst.

Neither Ish nor Ishshah (Adam nor Eve) understood what was occurring, nor did they need to. Instinct took over, beginning with Adam. It had to begin with him because he was the one who was now incomplete and thus compelled to move toward completion. (Eve? She simply stood there.) Consumed now with what the world has since learned to call "passion," Adam followed *talah* toward the cause of its awakening. He was intrigued, himself, to see what could possibly happen next.

When the nearness of a woman arouses a man today, what does he instinctively long for? A reuniting with his missing rib? Ah, but the male anatomy is smarter than the "brilliant" translators of our common Bibles. "Rib" illuminates nothing and takes us nowhere. Do a man's ribs begin quivering when he notices an attractive female? Please. What *does* move, however, is the thing that fits perfetly into the thing that Adam lost. What a coincidence. The right translation of *tsela* brings us a beautiful, sensible and physically demonstrable understanding of man, woman, and God. "And the two shall become one flesh." *Talah* knows what's missing, and it instinctively longs for the old neighborhood. In the marriage embrace, *talah* and *tsela* find happy reunion; this is an understatement. Humanity under the sheets is in a small measure whole again. It is a divine parable of how all humanity will one day rise and go forward together toward reunion with God.

Men today in the throes of sexual reconnection report a longing to crawl inside their *ishshah,* to be consumed by her. This is normal and not unexpected. It is consistent with the parable of humanity's ultimate consummation. But today we see only dimly into this coming world. God is content for now with a microcosmic picture, graciously allowing us six inches into the kingdom.

It is a pledge of greater things to come.

So-called fetishists

I think it is a good time now to pause, take a deep breath, and conduct a practical demonstration of the aforementioned truths. I wish for all male readers, therefore, to go into the bathroom and lock the door. Make sure that no children are hiding behind the shower curtain; check behind the shower curtain very carefully. Everything kosher? Then read on.

Get your wife's hand mirror, take off your clothes, and grab the loose skin around your scrotal sac. No questions at this point, please, just do as I say. Go back and test the lock on the bathroom door, to make certain that it works. Check behind the shower curtain one more time. Lock engaged? No children in the tub? Then you're ready to proceed.

Spread your legs apart and bend slightly forward while pulling your scrotal sac up against the front of your body, out of the way. Are you comfortable? If so, then you're not doing this properly. Please try again.

Hold your wife's mirror face up between your legs, just above knee level. You are preparing to examine your own perineum, of course. Anything more than this I cannot now tell you. Anyone wishing additional information must proceed to the next paragraph.

Adjust the mirror until the intersection of your anatomy comes into view. Now confirm this for me, that running north to south underneath you, from the base of your scrotal sac to the place where your undigested food disembarks, is a dark line that looks like an old suture scar. You saw this most obviously the last time you changed the diaper on a baby boy. All males, from crib to grave, have this line. Women do not have it. What is it? It is a genetically transmitted remnant (a scar, if you will) of the most sublime operation ever performed upon the human race. It is the place where God removed *tsela* from Adam to make Eve.

Note the precise wording from the Concordant Version of Genesis 2:21—"And taking is He one of his angular organs and is closing the flesh under it."

God closed the flesh *under* the organ. The Hebrew word translated "under" is *tachath.* The Concordant Version translates it correctly. The King James Version, however, translates it "instead," a word that in other contexts might fit, but which here fails miserably. Read this passage from the KJV and see if "instead" makes sense: "And He took one of his ribs, and closed up the flesh instead thereof." He closed up the flesh instead of *what* thereof? Instead of leaving it flapping in the wind? Instead of closing up the rib?

Stranger yet is discovering that the KJV renders *tachath*

correctly in Exodus 32:19. In this context, Moses breaks the tablets of stone "beneath the mount"—speaking of Mount Sinai. Why not make it "instead" here? The translators got handcuffed by the context. Moses breaks the tablets of stone *instead* of Mount Sinai? That was too ridiculous even for the King James translators.

Since the translators made *tachath* "beneath" here, why didn't they do it in Genesis 2:21? Because it did not fit their rib theory.

It is assumed and passed along as fact by many orthodox Christians that men have one fewer rib than women. But this is a fairy tale; ask any doctor or anatomist. Both men and women each have two pairs of ribs, twelve on each side, making a grand total of twenty-four. If men had only twenty-three, don't you think the orthodox Christians would be making a bigger deal of it? Don't you think they'd be publicizing x-rays showing the male's missing rib? This would be valuable evidence in convincing unbelievers of the veracity of the Genesis account. When consistently translated, the Genesis account is certainly true, but the truth is discovered via locks and mirrors, not x-rays.

The most startling *Rolling Stone* cover I've ever seen was the one dated January 22, 1981, featuring the famous Annie Leibovitz photograph of John Lennon and Yoko Ono lying on a plain white mattress. Lennon is naked, lying on his side in the fetal position, left leg atop a supine and fully-clothed Ono, knee pulled clear up to his left arm, which wraps itself around Yoko's face. John's face is buried into the side of his wife's, and he's passionately kissing her cheek. Yoko's arms are crossed up behind her head. She is not embracing Lennon. Her head is turned slightly and she looks away almost distractedly, comfortably accepting of, yet visibly unmoved by, John's passion.

I'm sure that many joyless and puritanical Americans turned quickly away from this cover after viewing it accidentally at Barnes & Noble booksellers. To them, it was probably "a disgusting display of human decadence," fit only

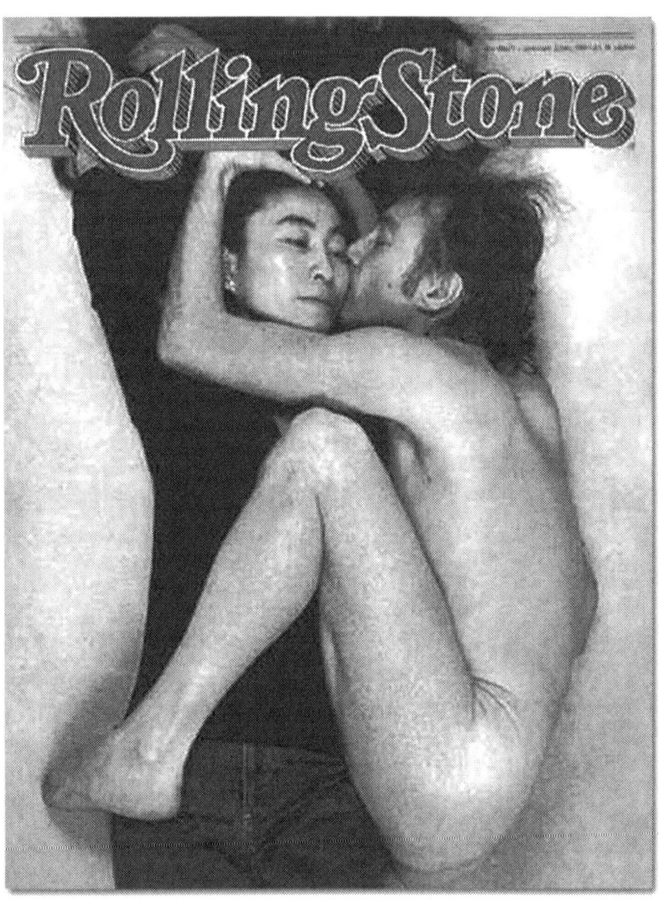

for the trash heap. How unfortunate. Had they viewed the cover with the eyes of God, they'd have beheld the nearest photographic evidence existent of what occurred in Eden between Adam and his wife at the dawn of human eroticism.

Genesis 2:24, "Therefore a man shall forsake his father and his mother and cling to his wife."

In the New Testament, the apostle Paul repeats this charge in Ephesians 5:31. This exhortation is given only to the husband. God never instructs wives to cling to their husbands, ever. This desperate drawing to the physical is an Ish trait. This is why I appreciate the fact that Yoko is clothed and John is naked. It emphasizes the disparity of physical need between women and men, which is a woman's ultimate advantage. I doubt that John and Yoko studied Genesis and Ephesians, and yet, looking at this *Rolling Stone* cover, could there be a better re-enactment of Scriptural truth?

Adam fell forward, not Eve. He moved toward her because he now had the lack. God robbed *him*, not her. He longed, she merely looked on. Nothing has changed. Men lose their minds while women gaze down at us, amazed. We fall forward, they do their nails and wonder what's the matter. Our sexual intensity mystifies most of them. They are not wired to do this. The depth of our pang for their form escapes them. Today's woman, assuming Eve's place, would have noted the desperately advancing man and said, "I've got everything *I* need; what's *your* problem?"

The woman's advantage over the man, which began in Eden, is her ability to keep her head while he loses his. I am not saying that women never lose it, but that men lose it sooner, faster, and with greater verve. In fact, men are so preoccupied with sex that a case can be made for them existing in various degrees of "losing it" all day long. The woman who recognizes this disparity as a gift of God rather than a perversion or a curse is well on her way toward marital bliss.

In the arena of passion, the weaker sex is the stronger sex because of the weakness of the stronger sex for the weaker sex. This is such an important sentence. Understand it wholly. Commit it to memory. It is yet another key to the kingdom.

The events of Eden explain much, such as the sight orientation of males. Even in cartoons, the eyeballs of men pop from their heads on springs when a beautiful cartoon woman walks into the room. The tongue of the cartoon male rolls from his mouth at a mere wink from "the other kind." Have you ever seen springs displacing the eyes of a cartoon *femme*? Have you ever seen an animated woman with tongue flapping like a Saint Bernard's? Does the animated woman go to pieces at the appearance of *ishus cartoonus*? Not even our most imaginative animators have been able to dream up these scenarios. Little do the animators realize what guides their colored pencils and how old it is.

Men have historically proposed to women on bended knee. They have bowed to kiss women's hands, spread coats over puddles for women to walk upon, died in battle protecting a woman's honor, dueled to the death with rival suitors for the favor of a woman's glance. Turn it around and try to imagine women doing any of these things either to or for men. Go on; do it. Go back to the beginning of the paragraph and transpose the genders. The very concept, to me, is appalling. A man's face has never launched a thousand ships.

Women are weaker physically than men—they are "weaker *vessels*" (1 Peter 3:7)—but that's the extent of their disadvantage.

To set up His startling lessons, God requires disparity. If David and Goliath are equally matched, where is the shocking headline in *Israel Today?* If Goliath wins, we yawn and turn to the sports page. When David wins, we want every detail. If Joseph starts off his political career in Egypt as anything besides an Israelite slave, how are we astonished when he assumes power?

If all air masses are created equal, where is the wind that drives turbines and keeps kites aloft?

When we impose a political correctness upon God's Word, that is, when we force equality into revelation to avoid some supposed moral affront, we engage in a kind of spiritual communism, robbing God of His greatest truths.

Men are not animals, and neither are they perverts. Men behave awkwardly when trying to explain their sex drives because many women's reactions to them have made them self-conscious and communicationally constipated. I want to encourage women to think more highly of themselves, for nothing could be more appropriate. But many women today have been taught that it's a sin to think highly of themselves, and therefore it must be a sin for men to react so strongly to them. Society—especially religious society—has degraded women for decades, centuries, millennia. Why is this so, if women are superior? It is so *because* women are superior. Men fear women; they always have. They fear their intelligence, their grace, their quiet power. But first and foremost, they fear their beauty. Certain cultures keep women robed and veiled because, above all else, men fear female flesh. They realize their powerlessness against it.

Men know that the female form is but the first weapon in a woman's vast arsenal. Should the entire arsenal be unleashed, women would become the societal chiefs and the men would work for *them*. The only way misguided men have historically been able to keep this from happening is by brute strength and unfair laws.

Women should take the years of subjugation as a backhanded compliment.

I don't mean that women are unsuited for rearing children. I consider child-rearing a woman's highest calling. I'm only arguing against the stereotype that women are suited *only* for this. To me, women managing corporations is a given: of course they can do it. I just hate seeing a superior gender striving for equality with men. In order to be equal with men, women must lower themselves. As Ronald Regan once famously remarked: "Women are superior to men, therefore equal rights will downgrade them." And so women are now equally hassled, equally harried, equally fighting traffic, equally shuffling papers, and equally enduring office politics. Are congratulations in order? Not from me. It could be that women needed to prove their prowess to themselves and to the world. Now that they've done it, I say they're smart to live like queens in a peaceful environment and have the men sweat and serve them.

What is a goddess? A goddess is served. A goddess is at spiritual and emotional leisure. A goddess is catered to by a man. Let the men fight dragons and kick copy machines. A man strives for cash, a goddess receives it from his hand. Who is the true superior: the woman who struggles to make a living, or the woman who has figured out how to get a man to struggle for her?

We come now to what women must consider the dark side of their gift, namely, that men objectify them; not only men, but society-at-large—specifically: advertisers. Check out the magazine rack at Wal-Mart today and see how many men grace the covers. Now, how many women? These women—are they wearing canvas potato sacks? Not unless you happen to be looking at *Idaho Farmer.*

Advertisers use female beauty to sell everything from curling irons to coffee pots to catalytic converters. Why? Because everyone likes women. Men like women; women like women; babies like women; dogs and cats like women; domesticated fish like women. Even houseplants admire the descendants of Eve. What's not to like? And yet I feel compelled to apologize for the male tendency to objectify. I did not invent the situation in Eden, but perhaps everyone will feel better after I've explained it.

Eve occupied a place beside the river Gihon where, before, there was nothing—at least nothing that looked like *this*. Adam went from "I know everything on this horizon," to "There is a new thing here between the earth and the sky." It was not Adam's fault, then, that he viewed Eve spatially at first, any more than it was Eve's fault that *everything* was new to her simultaneously. (I like the word "spatially," and prefer the derivative "spatialize" to "objectify" in describing the phenomenon of men seeing women first as objects.)

Adam was no marvel to Eve, no more than the trees on the bank and the kangaroo. Her first craving, then, would not have been for Adam's body, but for his knowledge. She needed to know where she was and how she got there. She

Sunshine
HiHo
CRACK

needed information, and sought it from the first thing that looked smarter than a coconut. The best bet was Adam; specifically, his eyes. *Here,* she thought, *are windows into a soul like mine.* And ever since, Eve's descendants have sought their soul mates—beginning above the neck.

Ask a woman today what is the first thing she notices about a man, and she will often say, "His eyes." Pose the same question to a man and the answer isn't worse, just different: "I notice her body. I notice all the physical ways she's different from me." He's telling the truth. It's the same thing his forefather did.

In the Song of Solomon—also known as the Song of Songs—both bride and bridegroom soliloquize over one another's physical charms. In chapter 5, the bride lists ten physical things that she likes about her groom, and the groom reciprocates in chapter 7, soliloquizing over her.

Note the chart on the facing page. On the left are listed those physical traits of the bridegroom cherished by the bride. On the right are the first things the groom notices about her. The order of the things listed is neither coincidental nor inconsequential; nothing in Scripture is. Rather, it's inspired.

First on her list is his head. From here, she works down. He, on the other hand, begins at her feet, and works up. She does not arrive below his neck until point six, at the same time he finally ventures north of her breasts. Remarkable! And yet it isn't. It's typical of the God-given differences between the sexes.

The bride first wants her lover's thoughts and emotions, and so begins at the seat of his intellect. He, on the other hand, wants to cling to and worship her femininity, and for him that begins at her feet. It's perfect; symbiotic; instinctual—wonderful! Each gender fulfills its role.

All men should begin the courting process at a woman's feet, either figuratively or literally. Preferably literally. Men eventually arrive here when proposing marriage, but what took them so long? A man at a woman's feet is a physical act, but simultaneously symbolic. The Lord Jesus Christ literally washed the feet of the disciples, but who cannot see, behind the performance, an act of humility, sacrifice and service?

It would stun a modern woman to see a man bowed down before her. Even the propositioned woman giggles and turns red at the suitor on bended knee. This is not the case for the woman aware of God's role for her. It is not in her to giggle or blush. She knows her power and its effect. Here it starts. From this vantage point, a woman gazes upon a man's head and locks. How patient is the bride of Solomon. As Solomon's worship ascends, she seeks the windows to his soul. At her navel, he gazes up at her in adoration. Their

Song of Songs 5:11-16		Song of Songs 7:1-5	
She loves his (in order):		**He loves her (in order):**	
1. head 2. locks 3. eyes 4. cheeks 5. lips	**Above the neck; top to bottom**	1. feet 2. hips 3. navel 4. belly 5. breasts	**Below the neck; bottom to top**
6. hands 7. abdomen 8. legs 9. appearance 10. mouth		6. neck 7. eyes 8. nose 9. head 10. hair	

paths cross at point 6; he is rising now and his strong hands caress her neck. He rises to full stature as her eyes now descend the corrugations of his trunk. Now he admires her beautiful head; he smells her hair.

At last, there is a kiss; she obtains the sweetness of his mouth. Like wine, the kiss has aged, becoming finer for the waiting. Four verses later, he soliloquizes over it: "Your mouth is like the best wine."

A young girl I know sees these principles plainly with her new boyfriend.

"He can't take his eyes off my body," she says.

I ask, "Is that bad?"

"I want a relationship," she says.

"How long have you known him?"

"Two weeks."

"Give it time. He'll work his way to your soul. But for him, this is where the attraction starts."

"Where?"

I pointed to her low-cut jeans.

"In my belly button?"

"Your *figure,* Jeannine. You have a wonderful figure."

"I want a spiritual oneness with Ryan."

"You're assuming he doesn't?"

"He does believe in God."

"Then he'll get there. The phrase 'opposite sex' didn't come out of nowhere. Women go to the soul first, then the body. For men, the body is the conduit to the soul."

"That sounds profound. But hey, I'm *not* having sex with him."

"I'm not talking about jumping in the sack. Ryan is infatuated with your packaging; this is a good thing. Sex isn't just 'doing it' with somebody. It's the fullness of the energy. There's energy between you, right? I mean, you don't seem too upset that Ryan's a football player. The guy's got great arms."

"Oh, I love Ryan's body. I just want to make sure that he loves me for *me*."

"Then gain forty pounds. Stop washing your face. Contract acne. Chop your hair off. Dress in a bag. Wear Army boots."

"*Huh?*"

"Grow a mustache, Jeannine. Chew Skoal and overhaul a Chevy. Then you'll know for sure if he loves you for *you*."

"Hey! What are you trying to hand me?"

"Just a clue, Jeannine. Just a clue."

Adam knew everything alive along the banks of the Gihon; it was his business. So when he awoke from his sleep, the new creature calling his name commanded attention. He sees her first as a creature—a created thing. She took up what was once empty space. I apologize to womanhood for how this sounds, but it's simply how it was. The outward frame of a woman is not all men want, but it is how men begin to discover all that a woman is.

What were the fleshy mounds at the region of the chest? They fascinated Adam and he stared at them. *His* chest wasn't like that. Next, where *talah* should have been, was a dark place of—what? The talahic void of the woman mesmerized him. And why was this creature's hair so much

longer than his? He stared at the length, enthralled by it. He stared in a reverie, from her breasts, down to her mystery, then to the tresses tumbling out and over her smoother-than-his skin. No male since has enjoyed such unfettered staring. (Well, except perhaps for King Solomon.)

Adam didn't need a mirror to know that he was straight as a plumb line from his chest to his belly. Where he was a specimin of thoracic uniformity, there were spaces down either side of Eve; these spaces formed a curve. Was this ever different! Men have worshipped this curve ever since.

Surveys have proven that a waist/hip ratio (WHR) in women between .67 and .80 is to men what peanut butter is to the mouse: bait. This magical WHR is of divine invention. It is arrived at by dividing the circumference of the waist by that of the hips. A lower number indicates a greater difference. A reading of .67 starts men to stuttering. Sociologists have transported photographs of different WHRs of variously-sized women into jungles and asked the native males to point out their preferences. "Me like *that* one," is the universal response to the lower-ratioed women.

What is important, apparently, is not the leanness or obesity of a woman, but the presence of the ratio. This should come as good news to all women, because women typically possess ratios in this range. If you're an overweight female and cannot even attain the high-end number (.80), don't worry. The main thing is your lack of *talah* ("hanging"). This indicates overall feminine health, and you will attract lots of men.

My point is that men love differences.

The feminine curve is a widened pelvic region allowing women the capacity to bear children. Evolutionists claim that, due to some marvel of natural selection, men instinctively choose women in the aforementioned range. Darwin says that males learn over time to choose wide-hipped women because these are most able to bear them children. *The wider the hips, the bigger the "nursery," and the better I'll be able to "stock the pond"* is what Darwin thinks men think in the depths of their double helices. (Let us all now observe a moment of silence, so that we may follow it by laughing our heads off.)

What utter stupidity. I don't think King Solomon was thinking about babies when he wrote the following of his beloved Shulammite: "O princely daughter! The curves of your hips are like jewels, the work of the hands of an Artist" (Song of Songs 7:1).

The Artist was God. The Shulammite was Solomon's proxy god.

God had a dual purpose when designing a woman's hips. The extra width would accommodate offspring, that's true, but the first function of the hips was to capture a man. Which came first, the chicken or the egg? Adam had to be attracted to Eve before babies were even possible, and somebody forgot to tell him about natural selection. Reproduction is not the primary function of sex. Long after babies are possible, the descendants of Adam still fall for the magical flair of the female hip.

Fetishism is the art of finding sexualness in things. Men become aroused, for instance, when they see a woman's high-heeled shoe. This is completely natural. At least, King Solomon thought it was. Listen to what the wise man says of his bride in Song of Songs, 7:1, "How lovely are your sandaled footsteps, O princely daughter." That's from the *Concordant Version of the Old Testament*. The NASB is stupendous here: "How beautiful are your feet in sandals."

As the bridegroom ascends in his worship, he smells his loved one's clothing: "The scent of your raiment is like the scent of Lebanon" (Song of Songs 4:11), he says. In this distant day, we cannot know exactly how Lebanon smelled, but it must have smelled pretty good.

I remember several years ago when Heather, one of my wife's girlfriends, came up several panties short on laundry day. Then it happened again. And again. Turns out there was an old man with a young man's heart living next door who would sneak into Heather's basement on Wednesdays, steal her pre-washed underthings, then whisk them to his lair for further inspection. The man was eventually caught and sentenced to three weeks hard labor at a Fruit of the Loom factory/boxer division. The man became every local woman's enemy. "Pervert!" they called him. "Thief!" "Neanderthalic Taker of Heather's Panties!" To the local men, however, he was "Hero!" a man whose daring we heralded openly among ourselves, through tears. We understood the guy. Solomon would have, too.

I have yet to hear of a woman stealing a man's briefs, then returning to her boudoir for oral/nasal Jockey sex. The marvel does not exist. That it does not exist makes me wonder if men and women are essentially different. Could it be that God meant for male fetish power to be tapped by the fair sex? What energy here, and what potential for work if put to practical use.

Why is fetishism almost exclusively a male trait? Go back to Eden and Adam's initial infatuation with the physical. Men love the physical woman so much that her essence, for them, spills over onto her things. I can't think of how to say it any better, so I'll let Solomon do it—

> You have made my heart beat faster, my bride; you have made my heart beat faster with a single glance of your eyes, *with a single strand of your necklace* (Song of Songs 4:9).

Ever hear what Freud dreamed up on this?

The famous Austrian neurologist Sigmund Freud introduced something called the Oedipus Complex into our psychiatric vocabulary. Oedipus was a character of Greek legend who unwittingly killed his father and married his mother Jocasta.

Freud traced the source of fetishism to the supposed childhood desire of males to sleep with their mothers and kill their fathers. He said that, before they know any better, little boys think everybody has a penis. When a little boy finds out that his mother, specifically, doesn't have one (a thing more traumatic to him than discovering there's no Santa Claus) he averts his eye in horror, shouting, "Who took Mummy's wee-wee?" This so traumatizes the child that the first inanimate object on which the boy focuses (after averting his eyes) becomes the fetishized object, whether it's a yo-yo, a frying pan, or the latest issue of *TV Guide.*

After this, the boy learns to hate his father because he really wants to date his mother, who has no penis. He now becomes afraid that his father will cut his testicles off, which is known in Freudian folklore as "castration anxiety."

Um, o-*kay.*

Ish sniffed Ishshah's fig leaf—so what? Solomon took giant whiffs of his bride's see-through tunic—naturally. The king's heart palpitated as he stared at a single strand of her necklace—good for him/good for her. It's the power of association. It's the same reason you think of your grandmother when you ogle and nasally imbibe of a cherry pie.

Fetishist.

The celestials looking in

There were heavenly beings existent at the creation of Earth. God said to Job:

> Where were you when I founded the earth? Tell if you know with understanding. Who determined its measurements—for surely you know! Or who stretched out a measuring tape upon it? On what were its sockets sunk? Or who directed its cornerstone in place, when the stars of the morning were jubilant together, and all the sons of God raised a joyful shout?
>
> —*Job 38:4-7*

These sons of God—powerful, celestial beings—attend every new move of the Deity. This is why the apostle Paul said—

> For we became a theater to the world and to angels and to humans.
>
> —*1 Corinthians 4:9*

To celestial creatures, human beings are actors and actresses in a literal stage production. We are the real-life version of *The Truman Show.* In this film, actor Jim Carrey portrayed a man living an ordinary life, unaware of the gaze of invisible viewers. The apostle Paul revealed to the human race unknown levels of grace (Ephesians 3:2). This was Paul's special message: *grace.* Earth had never known such divine favor. Here was a message, not just for Israelites, but for everyone—especially sinners; especially losers. Such a spectacle was utterly more watchable than any Jim Carrey performance—as much as I like Jim Carrey performances. Even now, human beings known corporately as the body of Christ are "[making known] to the sovereignties and authorities among the celestials...the multifarious wisdom of God" (Ephesians 3:10).

They are watching us. They have never seen God bestowing such favor on such unworthy characters, for "the stupidity of the world, God chooses" (1 Corinthians 1:27).

Was it Paul's worthiness as a soldier of Christ that stunned the heavenly populace? No. It was the depth of his sin contrasted with the message of grace entrusted to him that rattled the celestial audience and riveted them to their viewing stations. On the day Christ called Saul (God changed his name later to Paul), Saul was a raving lunatic en route to Damascus to kill Christians. It was the contrast of Paul's ignobility set against the grace—*this* is what arrested celestial eyes. God could and should have struck Saul dead. Instead, He granted him the deepest gaze ever into the divine heart.

God's universal law is this: *the lower one sinks, the higher one rises in subsequent glory.* It is true of us, and was certainly true of Christ—

> [Christ] humbles Himself, becoming obedient unto death, even the death of the cross, *wherefore*, also, God highly exalts Him...
>
> —*Philippians 2:8-9*

God plunges us into death and life, darkness and light, evil and good. Without evil, however, appreciation of good is impossible. This is the purpose of all evil: contrast. (God is doing this *for* us, not *to* us.) He is preparing us for eternal happiness, but the only thing that can buy such a blessing is temporary misery. This is how it is for creatures dependent on contrast for revelation. This is how it must go.

Appreciate the universe-changing contrast into which God plunged Christ: *divinity vs. death on a Roman cross.* How is that for contrast? *Clothed in glory vs. naked on a cross—and then, upon resurrection, even greater glory than before.* My God. No contrast has ever been sharper or more profound. This act will never be repeated, thank God. But has there been no further demonstration of such contrast since Calvary—not even in microcosm?

Oh, there has. Millions of times a day, all over the world, humans enact just such a contrast to one or another degree. According to *The Penguin Atlas of Human Sexual Behavior,* 166,666 people around the world have sex every minute. Like the dawn symbolizing the good that conquers evil, and the Spring symbolizing the life that conquers death, sexual intimacy continually demonstrates, to the celestial host, a willing, non-lethal abandonment of one being to another, that is, of a lesser (male) to a greater (female). We strip naked only before doctors and sex partners—and the celestials don't give a damn about doctors.

Sex is a relinquishing of power. It is a naked vulnerability, lit for viewing. It sweats, writhes, and bites its lower lip—sometimes unto blood. Abandoning conscious thought, sex hurtles toward that which inexorably draws it. The cross—*the* Passion—was much like this. Sweat, and even pain, confronts a coming ecstasy. In so vulnerable a state, sex should be mortified. Instead, it throws itself wider apart; it cannot spread far enough, or become more exposed. Are the accompanying cries those of trauma or of ecstasy? *Both.*

> For the joy lying before Him, [He] endures a cross. —*Hebrews 12:2*

The celestials gasp at this divine parable. We, on the other hand, smoke cigarettes.

The secret of marriage (Ephesians 5:25-33) is the only secret in Scripture that Paul calls "great." How, then, can it not be a source of prime celestial theater? Especially in light of the following—

> The woman is the glory of the man. For man is not out of woman, but woman out of man. For, also, man is not created because of the woman, but woman because of the man. Therefore the woman ought to have authority over her head because of the angels.
>
> —*1 Corinthians 11:7-10*

The first fifteen verses of 1 Corinthians chapter 11 discuss a woman's literal head and what covers it. Strange? To us, yes. Who could possibly care? The celestials do. A woman's hair astounds them. Unlike us, they grasp the symbolism.

In the days before the first couple sinned, God gave Eve tresses instead of clothing (1 Corinthians 11:15). This pictures for the universe the protection due woman. As the glory of the man, woman brings to the man a favorable opinion that he would otherwise lack. For this, he is to cherish and protect her.

For centuries, women have suffered abuse from their male heads. The covering of hair or any artificial covering speaks, not of a woman's subjection *to* a man, but of her protection *from* him. (For more information on this important and misunderstood topic, see my book, *Eve Raised*.) The covering lends her a degree of autonomy beneath the man that not even the man possesses beneath Christ. Beneath Christ, the man must *not* cover (1 Corinthians 11:4), but must rather be relatively naked before Him.

A husband remains his wife's head, yet his influence over her is less than that of Christ's over him. He is not to dominate, but to protect her. The celestial beings long to see this. A woman's tresses picture for the celestial citizens this protection, even in the face of male failure. I wish more men would succeed. I wish more men would consider women to be better than themselves—because they are. Perhaps now that I've initiated male readers into celestial interest and feminine worth, more men will go the extra mile to protect and serve women. Not even a man holding open a door for the fair sex escapes heavenly notice.

If the beings above glean so much from a woman's tresses and the mere opening of a door for her, what do they learn from the greater manifestations of sexual attraction? From the quickened heartbeat? His stolen breath? Her pinched, sweet cries? His nakedness bent before sublime beauty? Her nails tearing him? The pained ecstasy? The clutch? His face? How she lifts him with her hips? The lights beneath his lids? Male essence, withdrawn? The crying out to God?

Square dancing.

Woman as proxy god

We are taught to picture God as an old man with a white beard. No description of Him could be further from the truth; God does not resemble Merlin the Magician. God is not a man, and neither does He resemble one. God Himself is invisible; He is spirit (John 4:24); spirit is His essence. Yet His essence is the most beautiful thing imaginable. We cannot see God, but we behold, day by day, that which has come from Him, that is, His creation.

Notice in Genesis the progressive nature of God's creation. He begins with plants: azalea bushes, sunflowers, wheat, grass, elm trees, and dandelions. He then fills the seas with living, moving souls: plankton, starfish, crabs, scallops, seals, and the giant sperm whale. The sperm whale is a step up from the dandelion—somewhat. The celestial citizens, beholding all this, marvel at God's power.

Without stopping, God then populates the near heavens with various flying things: eagles, hawks, wrens, and the yellow-bellied sapsucker. The sapsucker surely stupefied the celestial worldmights, who no doubt supposed it to be God's *pièce de résistance.*

They were wrong about that.

Next from God's hand came the life that crawls upon land: ants, porcupines, warthogs, elephants, and cats. Ah, now we have it. Surely with cats God had exhausted His creative genius.

But no.

On day six, God created Adam. As Adam arose from a pile of mud, a hush befell heaven. Before the gaze of all stood a being of reason and wonder, able to kneel and sniff the soil in awe at its own quintessence. *At last, the ceiling.*

Well, not so fast. Surely heaven caught its collective breath as Eve ascended to full height, dressed in a halo of morning mist. What wide, smooth hips. *Her legs! My God! They're longer than the gazelle's!* Birds must have alighted upon her, while butterflies flitted to her hair. The piano had yet to be invented, but whatever celestial instrument prefaced it struck gorgeous tones. For here was not merely another human, but an improved specimen.

In our modern language, Eve was Adam 2.0.

The celestial attendants looked at God, then at Eve; then at God, then at Eve; then at God, then at Eve; God, Eve, God, Eve—on it went. With the thousandth pass, light dawned. Adam mirrored God's strength, but here, in the woman, the celestial world perceived God's crushing beauty.

As did the first man.

Woman is proof, upon the Earth, of the irresistible gorgeousness of God.

> Therefore a man shall forsake his father and his mother and cling to his wife, and they two become one flesh.
>
> —*Genesis 2:24*

Who was Adam's father? God. What became of Him? With the entrance of sin, God withdrew. Parabolically—in the absence of direct divine contact—Eve becomes a proxy-god and Adam her worshipper. I already talked about this, but you need more of it. This truth seems astounding, I know. Paul later writes:

> The unmarried one is solicitous about the things of the Lord, how he should be pleasing the Lord. Yet he who marries is solicitous about the things of the world, how he should be pleasing his wife, and is parted.
>
> —*1 Corinthians 7:32-33*

It is wrong, in a marriage, to be undistractedly for the Lord. The wedded are to part from the Lord—in part—and be joined to one another. From now on, they are to be preoccupied with the sexual arts—

> Yet because of prostitutions, let each man have a wife for himself and each woman have her own husband. Let the husband render to the wife her due, yet likewise the wife also to the husband. The wife has not the jurisdiction of her own body, but the husband, yet likewise the husband also has not the jurisdiction of his own body, but the wife. Do not deprive one another, except sometime it should be by agreement for a period, that you should have leisure for

prayer, and you may be the same again, lest Satan may be trying you because of your incontinence.

—1 Corinthians 7:2-5

The sexual absorption must be such that, in order to talk to God, husband and wife must consciously halt the preoccupation with their bodies. How can this be when the sexual encounter itself is so brief? The sacred relation is more than corporeal function; it is a power exchange occurring continually. Its nature as a parable requires unceasing recognition. Thus, we cannot limit its application to the physical aspects. If sex is but an act, who needs prayer as an excuse for leisure? The act itself demands a recuperative interval. This is not so of sexual *energy.* The exchange of power exists—or should exist—long before and long after the act itself. In fact, it should continue uninterrupted until the couple realizes that they have *over*-neglected the Maker of their bliss.

Do not suppose that the Lord feels robbed by marital sex. He knows that husband and wife are parted from Him for a high purpose. The couple, having wed, embarks upon a life of parable necessary to themselves, to God, to Christ, and to the attending celestial host. God is fine with it; He invented it. The intimate life not only fulfills the respective participants, but demonstrates to the world and the universe-at-large two great truths:

- A husband's going toward and clinging to his wife pictures humanity as a whole going toward and clinging to God.

- A husband's desire to suffer (physically) and sacrifice (to nurture and cherish) for his wife pictures Christ's suffering

and sacrificing for the ecclesia, that is, the church which is His body.

Let's explore this latter aspect. In Ephesians 5:32, Paul calls it the secret of marriage—

> Husbands, be loving your wives according as Christ also loves the ecclesia, and gives Himself up for its sake, that He should be hallowing it, cleansing it in the bath of the water (with His declaration), that He should be presenting to Himself a glorious ecclesia, not having spot or wrinkle or any such things, but that it may be holy and flawless. Thus, the husbands also ought to be loving their own wives as their own bodies. He who is loving his own wife is loving himself. For no one at any time hates his own flesh, but is nurturing and cherishing it, according as Christ also the ecclesia, for we are members of His body. For this "a man shall leave his father and mother and shall be joined to his wife, and the two shall be one flesh." This secret is great: yet I am saying this as to Christ and as to the ecclesia. Moreover, you also individually, each be loving his own wife thus, as himself, yet that the wife may be fearing the husband.
>
> —Ephesians 5:25-33

The manner in which Christ emptied Himself was graphic.

> For let this disposition be in you, which is in Christ Jesus also, Who, being inherently in the form of God, deems it not pillaging to be equal with God, nevertheless empties Himself, taking the form of a slave, coming to be in the likeness of humanity, and, being found in fashion as a

> human, He humbles Himself, becoming obedient unto death, even the death of the cross.
>
> —*Philippians 2:5-8*

Paul is talking about a *disposition* of sacrifice here, and not a literal re-enactment of *Christ's* sacrifice. Christ gave Himself up for the sake of the ecclesia by suffering and dying for it. This was His particular sacrifice. It is not the husband's sacrifice. A husband follows the example of sacrifice, not by being crucified, but by nurturing and cherishing his wife. It is a sacrifice for the husband to love someone other than himself. Women easily do this; men have a harder time of it. While Paul puts forth Christ as an example of One Who sacrificed, the sacrifice asked of husbands is certainly not Christ-specific. It is Christ-*like*, but not Christ-specific. It is in Ephesians 5:28-29 where Paul specifically describes the kind of "giving up" to which husbands are exhorted: "Thus, the husbands also ought to be loving their own wives as their own bodies. He who is loving his own wife is loving himself. For no one at any time hates his own flesh, but is nurturing and cherishing it."

This nurturing and cherishing of wives by husbands is the obvious point of Paul's comparison. Christ was so powerful that He could have destroyed the ecclesia with a single swipe. Instead, He gave Himself up for the ecclesia, hallowing and cleansing it. Thus, husbands—who are much stronger than their wives and can easily hurt them—are to instead nurture and cherish them. That's that. Paul is not directly telling us anything more.

Let us now, however, consider the not-so-obvious. Let us consider the extreme, *physical* aspects of Christ's sacrifice in order to detect a possible correlation between these and the more extreme physical aspects of sexual relations.

The literal intersection of bodies and passions (that is, physical sex) invites and fulfills extremities of both female and male desire. The physical desire and esteem of a husband for his wife can and oftentimes does (in either small or great measure) graphically tap the literal elements of Christ's passion. As far as I am aware, crucifixion is illegal in most states. Short of that, however, males and females/husbands and wives may, in measure—and yet to impressive degrees—reproduce the point-by-point sacrifice of Christ on the day that He died. The celestials require pictures, and pictures they get. They require pictures—not theories—of so great an emptying as our Lord's; the secret of marriage touches both sex *and* the cross. It touches both pleasure *and* pain; it's both emotional *and* physical—the physical acted out in various bedrooms and chambers on the great stage of Earth. The aforementioned physicalities—some small, some large—hearken to the most graphic examples of humility and endurance ever recorded—

> [They] gave Him slaps.
>
> —*John 19:3*

> My back I give over to smiters, and My cheeks to those who tear at My beard; My face I do not conceal from mortification and spitting.
>
> —*Isaiah 50:6*

> Then Pilate took Jesus, and whips Him.
>
> —*John 19:1*

> Yet He was wounded because of our transgressions, and crushed because of our depravities. The discipline of our well-being was on Him, and with His welts comes healing for us. —*Isaiah 53:5*

> Yet Yahweh desires to crush Him, and He causes Him to be wounded. —*Isaiah 53:10*

Curiously (I would rather say "logically"), a billion-dollar, global industry exists to accommodate millions of men who want/need to pay women to physically do to them what the Romans did to Jesus. (For every man who steps across that threshold, thousands more secretly imagine it; I assume that most wives simply won't hear of it, don't understand it—or both.) I did not invent this phenomenon, and neither am I the first to notice it. I may, however, be the first to explain it.

Generally speaking, men, not women, appoint for themselves members of the opposing gender to test, with physical trial, their loyalty to and worship of them. (Consider the "days of yore" when knights courted ladies and competed for them with various, manly trials.) Christ willingly endured radical pain for His beloved ecclesia. It's the extremity of the affliction that impresses otherworldly onlookers. Am I saying that the celestials still watch it? They can and do. They marvel, still, at such endurance for the sake of such love. Why should the celestials watch re-runs of Mel Gibson's messy film when sex-disposed human beings line up voluntarily for the privilege and thrill of Calvary-like drama? Do the human beings know what they're doing? Of course not—perhaps not until now. It's instinctive. But what two greater physical intensities

exist here on this planet besides sex and crucifixion? Don't shoot the messenger; I am not the One Who first compared Jesus Christ to husbands.

> Because of prostitutions, let each man have a wife for himself and each woman have her own husband.
>
> —*1 Corinthians 7:2*

Paul makes it plain here—some would say painfully plain—that marriage is about sex. Men already know this. Women, it seems, are sometimes hesitant to believe it. As stated earlier, however, sex is more than intersecting body parts. It is a condition of the wedded atmosphere, constant as oxygen. Any two people can love Christ and each other. Any two people can sacrifice, one for the other. Those entering the marriage covenant, however, do these same things, yet under the umbrella of sex. That is the difference between marriage and platonic love. Marriage is a sex pact. Repeat: *marriage is a sex pact.* I wish it were called that more openly. The acknowledgment of this truth would save marriages; couples need to know what they're getting into.

Sex is a medley of both clothed and naked *acts.* Husband and wife—not man and woman, generally—enter the sacred world of coital tension where Christ and the ecclesia get graphically (that is, physically) illustrated. Husband and wife picture not only the drawing power of God upon humanity, but Christ's sacrificial emptying for the ecclesia (the husband nurtures and cherishes his wife), which is on some level sexual, otherwise mere men and women could accomplish it.

SEX ACT

Husband listens as wife speaks—SEX ACT
Husband opens car door for wife—SEX ACT
Husband rises early; works for wife—SEX ACT
Husband buys wife diamond—SEX ACT
Husband donates kidney to wife—SEX ACT
Husband takes bullet intended for wife and dies—SEX ACT

* * *

Wife confides to husband—SEX ACT
Wife waits for husband to attend to her—SEX ACT
Wife admires husband's work—SEX ACT
Wife receives diamond—SEX ACT
Wife accepts husband's kidney—SEX ACT
Wife accepts death of husband for her sake—SEX ACT

Of the four grand secrets of Ephesians, only one is called "great." This is the one (Ephesians 5:32).

The secret of marriage began—in embryonic form—at God's departure from Eden. It ends at the return of Christ. What need of parable when That which the parable symbolizes returns to Earth? Thus the Lord attests: "For in the resurrection neither are they marrying nor taking in marriage, but are as the angels of God in heaven" (Matthew 22:30).

Until then, God gives us a foretaste of the tree of life. In the marriage embrace, creation beholds a microcosmic picture of God and humanity, rejoined in the Garden. And on it goes, until the way to the tree is re-opened for the duration of time.

The worship of woman

I drove past our local high school around three o'clock last afternoon and saw a group of about six young men standing around a single girl. It's the nature of things. In the beehive, workers and drones toil ceaselessly for the queen. Upon the wall of the uterus, sperm and egg rehearse the drama of the high school parking lot: millions of anxious sperm surround a single egg. The sperm swim to, surround, and worship the egg; it mesmerizes them. The egg, unsatisfied, emits a chemical to attract even more single-tailed cells, drawing them like bugs to an electronic zapper. The egg at last admits a single fortunate suitor, then unleashes a potent chemical that kills the rest.

Honest men know that there is no word more appropriate than "worship" to describe the depth of their pang for womanhood. Most men cannot articulate this pang for fear both of the pang itself and of its rejection. Men do attempt to speak of it, but the words come hard and falteringly. They tiptoe into the arena of honesty, often to be shooed back—by women—as animals. Or perverts. Sinners, for certain.

Is it blasphemous to even think of womanhood in the same terms as Deity? No. God Himself made the parable. God is invisible, yet women walk among us. Beautiful women. The man would plead his case: *God! Why the tsunamic power of black lace against peach-colored flesh? Why lace at all? The rings of Saturn and the edge of delicate nightwear—What are you saying, Lord? Give me ears to hear.*

Many people think that a man must not worship a woman; he must worship only God. But the word "worship," like the word "love," goes many ways. One may love God, children, and strawberry cheesecake—without condemnation. Similarly, worship can apply to humans,

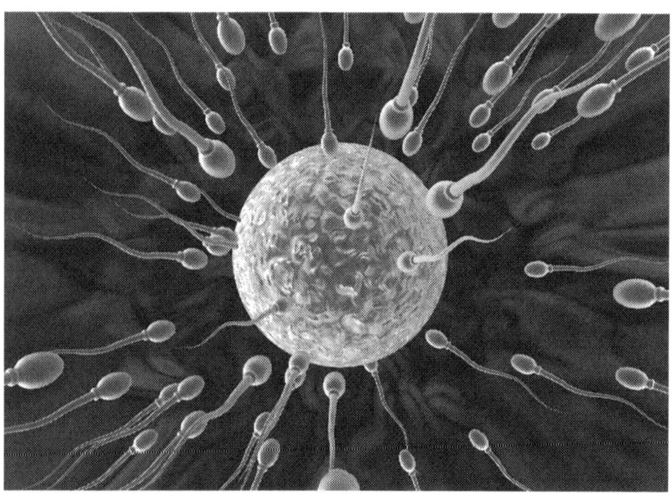

God, or deity-like desserts. We simply don't hear it as often. Worship applied to humans and things is rare, but no less legitimate. And yet it is condemned, generally, by the fair sex. I wonder why.

According to the dictionary, "worship" is the verb form of the adjective "worth." A woman is *worth* a great deal to a man, and she likes that. Strange, then, that she would disparage the verb. A woman's poor self-esteem allows her to hear a decaffeinated phrase such as, "I adore you," and stay calm. "I worship you" (basically, "I *worth* you"), however, is a double-shot of espresso in a white cup; it makes her nervous. Fearing that men have plunged over the precipice of idolatry, some women forbid such language.

To claim idolatry—as some women do when the adjective "worth" becomes the verb "worship"—is quite a feat for four letters of the alphabet (namely, "s," "h," "i," and "p").

Men have no intention of sacrificing goats to their wives—at least none of the men I know. British magistrates address one another as, "Your worship," and no one thinks a thing of it. Why can't we take the word at face value?

Love is an emotion arousing delight in and desire for the presence of its object. Worship, on the other hand, is a going toward that object with dog-like fawning. In Scripture, the Greek word translated, "worship," is *proskuneo*. Its literal English elements are "toward-teem." The word "teem" means, "to empty or pour out." To "toward-teem," then, is to pour out toward another person or thing, or toward God Himself.

Love is the emotion, worship the action.

We easily apply love to God, to a spouse, and to strawberry cheesecake, without confusing the three. No one thinks that the dessert is the spouse, or that the spouse is God, or that God is the dessert. No one of my acquaintance has ever said, "How dare you love strawberry cheesecake *and* God." People can love both—and often do—distinguishing them in the following manner: "This is God/This is strawberry cheesecake. *Got it.*" At least, none of my friends believe that strawberry cheesecake called Israel out of Egypt.

If you've ever watched *The Addams Family,* you've seen Gomez Addams worshipping his wife Morticia. To me, it's a beautiful thing. Gomez ravishes Morticia's arm—up and down, up and down—planting dozens of rapid kisses upon it. Morticia speaks one word of French, and off goes Gomez—off the deep end of Addamsian adoration. It's the French that does it to him. It isn't that Gomez does not always love Morticia. He loves her always, even when she speaks English.

Who wouldn't love Morticia Addams? She is the ultimate long cool woman in a black dress. But while the love exists, always, in the mind of Gomez, the emotion accompanying it lies dormant until provoked. For Gomez, Morticia's French brings that emotion to the fore and makes for memorable television.

Worship is a pouring out of dog-like fawning toward anything—anything at all. Even our Lord describes it pouring forth from one human being toward another, without a word of condemnation.

In Matthew 18:23-30, Jesus tells a parable about a man—a king—who wants to settle accounts with his slaves. One debtor comes forward in especially bad shape. This slave's debt is so large that he can't hope to pay it, so the king orders his wife and children confiscated. The slave begs the king for mercy. Jesus describes it this way—

"Falling down, then, that slave worshipped him."

The slave "toward-teemed" the king, pouring himself out, fawning over him like a dog. Love was absent in this case, but worship can stand alone. Jesus does not postscript His parable with: "The slave shouldn't have done that," or, "Only God should be worshipped." In Jesus' mind, there is no hint of idolatry on the part of the debtor; our Lord knew worship to be a generic word. He knew it could apply to God, to a spouse, to a king, or to any variety of cheesecake.

A misappropriation of Deuteronomy 6:13 has caused the confusion:

"The Lord your God shall you be worshiping, and to Him only shall you be offering divine service."

Our Lord repeats this saying in Matthew 4:10 and in Luke 4:8.

The first part of the verse, "The Lord your God shall you be worshiping," no more precludes one from worshipping strawberry cheesecake than "The Lord your God shall you be loving" precludes anyone from loving dogs, cats, or children. It is the second part of the verse—which adds an element to the worship of the context—that limits the worship of the context to Deity: "And to Him only shall you be offering divine service."

Note: "To Him *only* shall you be offering divine service." It is not that He must be worshipped exclusive of all else, but that He alone must be worshipped *and offered divine service to.* (That is, He is to be recognized as God.) Thus, while the first part of this verse allows anyone to freely worship strawberry cheesecake—and, say, the right arm of Morticia Addams—the second part precludes anyone from offering divine service to either the cheesecake *or* to Morticia Addams—much as one would like to.

Literature speaks frequently of "worshipful glances" (men toward women), but such male verve seems legal only in paperbacks of the romance variety. "He worships the ground she walks on," people say, and it has become such a famous figure of speech—and so quaint—that both sexes giggle at it.

I cannot join in the giggling. This worship business is too serious a thing to me. It touches too deep of a chord. It is socially acceptable to say it, I suppose ("he worships the ground she walks on"), as long as one refrains from lending the figure flesh. But what *then?* What if the male embodies it? What if the male, following the woman on his knees, kisses where her feet fall?

Is it perverted—or beautiful? The phrase is beautiful, but what of the practice? Is not the practice but the logical conclusion of the phrase? Could not God smile at such a wonder? Could not the Maker of ringed planets at least crack a satisfied grin?

God is invisible, and this galls me sometimes. God programmed humanity to worship Almightiness, but Almightiness, nowadays, does not wear skin. Can we be this honest with ourselves? And with God? The Deity today limits His personal appearances. The antidote is marriage and the two sexes. God created the sexes to give the angels a picture—and humanity an experience—of humanity at His feet. Each sex plays its part, and skin has a lot to do with it.

In the lush garden, God removed *tsela* (that is, the womb) from Adam to form a being Adam could cling to. God left in Adam a void that only Eve could fill. Adam lacked, but not so his wife. He went toward her, and not vice-versa. As stated earlier, even the anatomy testifies: the flesh of man rises toward the opposing structure, yet the essence of the woman slants inward, toward herself.

All goes toward Eve.

The proper term for this is: *worship*; in the Greek, "toward-teem." It is not worship of the woman as Deity, and neither is it homage given her instead of God. It is certainly not divine service. Rather, it is woman as conduit to a taste of the Almighty's celestial throne. A man on his knees before woman, then, tastes heaven. How does the woman arrive at these gates? By the receipt of male adoration. Her foretaste of heaven comes by receiving his homage.

It is symbiotic perfection.

Women deep down know their part of the parable. It is why they covet adoration and deep down need to be pedestalized. God made them this way. Denying it, they're unhappy. Admitting it, they're honest. Acquiring it, they're fulfilled. Men desire neither pedestalization nor worship from the opposing gender. Men want only permission to be what women need, for this is what *they* need. Men crave self-possessed, non-condemning proxy-gods who embrace their power and its consequence. Inhibition frustrates the parable; God wants it weepy and hot.

I would not know this for certain—no one can—but I believe that a male invented high-heeled footwear. From Eden on, it is the desire of men to pedestalize the better sex, and the elevated heel is an unconscious (or perhaps conscious) attempt at it. Elevated heels are mobile pedestals. A woman, wearing them, tacitly admits to every attending male: "I am worthy of your worship." She thus turns the heads of Adam's sons—even at construction sites—and returns them, in parable, to the uninhibited pleasures of Eden.

God once limited His presence to a small cubicle on Earth called the Holy of Holies—part of the ancient temple. Inside this cubicle was the Ark of the Covenant, containing the tablets of the law and the dead branch of an almond tree that continually blossomed. Golden cherubim—handcrafted angels—flanked this Ark. Moses fashioned the cherubim

with outspread wings, and between these wings dwelt a token of God's presence.

There was a light here, called the Shekinah glory. This was the token of God; it was light to see by. Visible light was physically impossible, as the room was surrounded by animal-skinned drapes. This light, therefore, was supernatural.

Only the high priest was allowed here—once a year, on the Day of Atonement—to sprinkle blood between the cherubim in atonement for the sins of Israel.

Preceding this was an oblong room, the Holy Place, containing an altar of incense, a candlestick, and a table containing twelve cakes of bread. Curtains draped this room as well.

Outside this lay the court, accessible to common clerics. There was an altar here, where men sacrificed living beasts, then burned the carcasses. There was a laver—a large pool of water—where priests ceremonially cleansed themselves.

As Israel approached God via the temple, thus also does humanity access heaven via a man's desire for the glorious sex.

The Holy of Holies represents, among other things, that part of a man that God removed to create woman. The womb is a woman's temple, wherein she receives the high priest. Behind her veils and curtains lies the Shekinah glory, an in-part presence and essence of Almighty God.

The cherubim on either side of the Presence figure, among other things, a woman's hips. A trained and sanctified priest rises to approach, but not without cost. There must first be blood and washing, sacrifice and cleansing. The Holy Place between the cherubim is earned, not given. Nothing comes near without preparation and training.

What is the aroma of the altar of incense except the scent of a woman and the nearness of the blessed consummation?

See the infatuation men have with that place, the desire to kneel before it and adore it; the desire to suffer for its sake. The skins of beasts, pulled taut against such supernal brilliance, lend erotic, suspenseful appeal to the ceremony.

Deep down, men want to suffer for women. They want an altar of sacrifice erected between themselves and the woman's glories. The woman who underrates herself devalues what God made her. Men build temples, not to glorify themselves, but to provide for themselves magnificence in which they can become but dust.

Many cultures pervert truth, and some have adopted goddess worship. In the forests, mountains and plains of strange places, women are worshipped as deities absolute. Obviously, this is not right. A culture perverting truth, however, does not negate it. There is something about women, and everyone knows it.

Our culture has perverted sex. Using it improperly for selfish ends, the "culture" has made some of our race embarrassed to be human. Few see the sacred parable.

Truth can be perverted, but never destroyed. The phrase, "In God We Trust," makes the all-seeing eye of the Deity (on our banknotes) touch all, even those hands that barter the bills for heroin. Likewise, in a million bedrooms; against lightposts; in the brothels of Amsterdam; in Fords and Chevies; under trees; on the beach, and between sheets of every fiber, The Parable, like the sun, shines on.

God never sleeps.

I wrote a novel, *Goddess of Nazareth*, about Joseph and Mary's intimate relationship. The earthly father of our Lord, possessor also of earthly passions, writes:

> Sun replacing night—it's so obvious to me now. The sun rising every day is God's picture of good conquering evil. No one needs an advanced education to appreciate it. The whole world sees it, but how many truly read it? Few, but it doesn't matter. It testifies. Somewhere deep in the liver or the heart, humanity suspects truth because of it. And God repeats the picture every single day of our lives. SUNRISE. *Get it?* SUNRISE. *Get it?* SUNRISE. *Get it?*
>
> *Shamat* ("sex") rules our world like the sun rules heaven. This moment, everywhere on Earth, passions run. Sweating bodies rise and fall, biles ascend into mouths to ecstasies of *Oh, God!* There! Did you hear it? Why do people call upon their Maker at the height of sexual ecstasy? Because deep down, humanity knows. Somewhere deep down, it knows. Man moving toward woman is a picture of humanity and God, and of how humanity moves as a race toward Him.
>
> The sexual climax is a parable of arriving home, of how it will feel when we finally leave this earth to join Him. It goes away so fast, but still, it's a picture. God has not left us bereft. He has given us a parable of what oneness with Him will feel like. OH, GOD! *Get it?* OH, GOD! *Get it?* OH, GOD! *Get it?*

* * *

The orgasm, then, is a half-ounce of how heaven will feel. The six inches man is allowed into woman pictures our race rising to meet its Maker. The climax, accompanying this, is a microcosm of how this will feel when it happens.

God creates lack and need. We suffer humiliations and pains in this world to prepare us for the next. Happiness there is impossible apart from misery here. Life's tensions only enhance the pull of glory, when at last it comes. In this way, God primes human desire. Women prime men, likewise, to make men prime *them*, to intensify the power of mutual release.

Sex is power play. Foreplay is power play. Foreplay is allegorical of an approaching Deity. Prior to the coming, God controls the intensity. In the allegory, women fulfill this. Women, not men, decorate sex. Women are to adorn themselves (1 Timothy 2:9; Proverbs 31:22; Revelation 21:2); this is never commanded of men. Women, not men, tease passion to perform.

I cannot speak for the female climax, but the male version is the ecstasy/agony of a soul exposed. It is male pride hurtling toward a precipice ensuring nudity. Male orgasm is the fear of death *and* life, forced to dance. It is the inability of pure muscle to cling for another moment to a thread of integrity. Male orgasm is enforced risk stirred to a tangible soup and flung without its consent toward celestial auditoriums. It is regret, delirium, repentance, joy—en route to a superior knowing.

It is rapture.

And so: women captivate; men vibrate; God celebrates; men and women come; Christ comes for us; cosmic explosions fill space, then as now. And the heavens and the Earth—all things evil and good—consummate into that from which all things came (Romans 11:36).

God.

Question and answer

Early in the book, you say that the male gender represents humanity and the female gender (meaning Eve) represents God. But later on, you say that man represents Christ.

This is the distinction between worship and service. The male gender does represent humanity—*up until Ephesians, chapter five.* Whenever we are considering humanity's motion Godward (as in Genesis), man represents humanity and woman represents God. This is worship. In Ephesians chapter five, however, we are considering a different thing, namely, Christ's motion manward, that is, toward the ecclesia. This is service. It is important to recognize these distinctions, for God Himself recognizes them.

You say woman represents God because she draws man and man goes toward her. I disagree. When left to itself, humanity does not go toward God. Rather, men

pursue their own ways. It is God Who takes the initiative and pursues man, woos man, offers man an "approach present" (Jesus Christ and Him crucified), etc. This is all typical of a man pursuing and wooing a woman. So it's the man who goes after the woman. *He* draws *her*. Therefore, the *man* represents God.

You combine "woo" and "pursue," as if they're synonymous. To woo, however, is *not* to pursue. It is to draw and let the object pursue. You speak as if man pursues woman without cause. You have forgotten why a man pursues a woman in the first place: *God makes women irresistible.* Sexual attraction starts with the woman, just as spiritual attraction starts with God. God does not run after man, but man after God. Why? Because God woos. It is active wooing, but wooing nonetheless. God draws humanity as a beautiful woman draws a man.

Jesus said, "No one can come to Me unless the Father Who has sent Me draws him" (John 6:44). Consider Romans 11:36—"All is out of God, through God, and into God." The key word here is "into." Creation moves into God, and not vice-versa. It is the same with men and women, respectively. Women draw, men move. Psalm 42:1 illustrates this well: "As a deer is panting over the channels of water, so is my soul panting for You, O Elohim."

I'll never forget reading Andrew Jukes' explanation of one of God's titles, El-Shaddai, in the book, *The Names and Titles of God*. The title El-Shaddai means, "Breasted One." A mother whose little one crawls toward a cliff, Jukes said, does not retrieve him by moving directly toward him, for that might startle him and cause him to fall. Rather, the mother

slowly yet purposefully exposes a breast. In the process of returning creation to Himself, God is more accurately typified by woman, not man. God is still the first cause.

Solomon knew the power of feminine charm, and warned his son, "Do not stray near the door of the strange woman" (Proverbs 5:8). Why the warning? What's so bad about a woman's door? This: the closer to the seductress his son gets, the stronger is her power and appeal, the more irresistible she becomes, and the harder it is for the boy to escape. Let's dress up this analogy a bit: the more God reveals Himself to us, the more irresistible He becomes. It is He Who draws: "All is *into* Him."

Concerning humanity's lack of spiritual interest, only a humanity completely bereft of spirit is thus afflicted. But no man is completely bereft of spirit. Paul said to the Athenian philosophers: "He makes out of one every nation of humanity, to be dwelling on all the surface of the earth, specifying the setting of the seasons and the bounds of their dwelling, for them to be seeking God, if, consequently, they may surely grope for Him and may be finding Him, though to be sure, not far from each one of us is He inherent" (Acts 17:26-27).

Who is groping for whom here? Think about it. Apply it to the analogy of woman and man. Who is the pursued, and who is the pursuer? Here is an unfortunate but appropriate analogy: In the workplace, who gropes whom?

In Scripture, God is always represented by the masculine gender. So how can women represent God in any way?

Surely you're not suggesting that God is a male. If He is a male, then He would also have to be a human being, which

He clearly is not. In 1 Samuel 15:29, the prophet testifies concerning God: "He is not a man." God is literally spirit (John 4:24). If God is not a male, is He a female? No. God is neither male nor female; He's genderless. Why, then, the pronoun, "He?"

The original languages of Scripture (Greek and Hebrew) assign to all nouns (including things) a gender; they are either masculine, feminine, or neuter. In the original languages, gender is a grammatical issue, not necessarily an issue of personality or *human* gender. For instance, the word Antioch (*Antiocheia* in Greek) is in the feminine gender. Does this mean the city is a woman? The word "stone" (*lithos*) is masculine. Is a stone a male? The word Christian (*Christianios*) is also masculine. Is a Christian woman therefore a man? If we were reading Greek, the pronoun would agree in gender with the noun to which it referred. Thus, Antioch would be "she." A man would point to a stone and say, "Look at *him*." "Christian" would always be "he" or "him," no matter the gender of the person.

In John 14:6, our Lord is called the Truth (*aletheia*) and the Life (*zoe*). Both words are feminine. Shall we therefore refer to Christ as *She* in these contexts? The Greek would demand it. In other contexts, however, Christ is called "Lord," or *Kurios*, in the Greek. This noun is masculine. Our Lord is in a gender crisis!

Our Lord did become a human being, and as such He was of the male gender. How do we know this if pronouns are so fickle? For one thing, He was circumcised the eighth day (Luke 2:21).

God, the Father of Christ, is a different matter altogether. That He is assigned gender at all is a figure of speech known as *anthropomorphia*, that is, ascribing to Deity what properly belongs to humanity. Since your argument that women cannot represent God depends on your perception of God as a male, your argument is negated.

Israel is always represented by the feminine gender. God, as her husband, is represented by the masculine. This disproves your teaching that woman represents God.

Israel is represented by the feminine gender only in its capacity as bride. The word Israel itself is masculine. Israel, son of Jacob, was a man, and the nation is named after him. In the case of the figure (Israel as bride and God as bridegroom), we are considering the covenantal relationship between God and the nation Israel—*only*. We are considering neither the drawing of humanity toward God, nor Christ's sacrifices on behalf of the ecclesia. Elsewhere in Scripture, Israel is referred to as grapes (Hosea 9:10) and a regressing vine (Hosea 10:1). Paul calls them boughs (as of a tree) in Romans 11:17, which is a masculine noun. By this you can surely see that, concerning Israel, there are different comparisons for different capacities. It's the same with God. When God draws humanity, woman represents Him. When God marries Israel, a bridegroom represents Him. When God speaks of His Son, a dove represents Him (Matthew 3:16). When He overshadows Israel, a cloud does the duty (Exodus 34:5). This for this, and that for that.

Man has the headship over woman as Christ has the headship over the church, and as God has the headship

P.C
1767

over Christ (and everything else). Therefore, the man is a representation of God while the woman is a representation of humanity.

Men exercising headship over women is not a Scriptural concept. What you mean to say is that husbands have headship over wives (Ephesians 5:22). Walk carefully. In Ephesians, man is not representative of God, as you state, but of Christ (Ephesians 5:25). Woman is not representative of humanity, but of the ecclesia (Ephesians 5:23-24). These are important distinctions. When God and humanity are in view, men represent humanity and women represent God. When Christ and the ecclesia are in view, men represent Christ and women represent the ecclesia. I plead for distinctions.

Humanity is the temple of God that God fills with His Spirit (seed). Woman has the temple (vagina/uterus) which man fills with his seed (sperm). That seed grows and produces fruit (children). God places His Spirit (seed) in us, which produces the "fruit of the Spirit."

You seem to intimate here that since God fills man with his spirit (seed) and produces fruit, and since man fills woman with his seed (spirit) and also produces fruit, therefore man is analogous to God, and woman analogous to humanity. You interpret seed as spirit, but Scripture never uses it this way.

In Scripture, "seed" is most often figurative and speaks of people; i.e. Abraham and his seed, the seed of David, the seed of Christ, land given to the seed, and so forth. The only passage of the forty or so New Testament usages where "seed" even approaches a metaphoric representation of spirit is 1 John 3:9—"Everyone who is begotten of God is not doing sin, for His seed is remaining in him, and he can not be sinning, for he is begotten of God." Even here, we are considering the progeny of God (that is, His offspring, conveyed by the word "begotten"), rather than that invisible power (spirit) that animates the progeny.

Let's apply the literal meaning and usage of seed to your analogy and see what happens; it is the literal usage and meaning, after all, upon which these figures are based. The literal meaning is, "that which is sown." We find its usage in 1 Corinthians 15:36-38—

> What you are sowing is not being vivified if it should not be dying. And, what you are sowing, you are not sowing the body which shall come to be, but a naked kernel, perchance of wheat or some of the rest. Yet God is giving it a body according as He wills, and to each of the seeds its own body.

Paul uses a literal seed to picture the bodies of believers. The topic of the passage is resurrection, and how the dead return to life. A literal seed is that which sacrifices itself (dies) in order to produce fruit. This not only describes seeds of grain and human bodies, but also—as you suggest—the male sperm. The millions of sperm "give it up" to undergo the long, treacherous passage to a woman's temple. All but one sperm die. In this analogy, humanity offers itself as a living sacrifice (seed) to God and produces the fruit of resurrection, while a man offers his living seed to his wife, and produces the fruit of children. In this

Scriptural analogy, man is analogous to humanity, and woman to God.

The vagina typifies the temple which God fills with His presence/Spirit, typifying communion/intercourse between God and man.

The vagina and uterus do, among other things, typify the temple. But this supports my contention, not yours. My contention, remember, is that woman represents God. This is true in the sphere of worship, and with the temple analogy we are entering that sphere. If the torn veil gave humanity access to God, which side of the veil represents God? Answer: the inner temple, which you rightly compared to the vagina/uterus. Yet you want to make man analogously God in this example, constantly filling the holy place. Since woman, to you, is typical of humanity, then you have humanity enthroned between the cherubim and God coming in from without. Are you sure you want to do that? God doesn't continually fill the temple; rather, the temple houses His continuous presence.

In our analogy, humanity/the high priest/the aroused husband—these all approach from without, seeking the holy presence. The torn veil comes at a cost to God and woman. And yes, "It is finished" aptly illustrates many things.

Your writings on men worshipping women are almost convincing. But why did angels and apostles forbid people to worship them? Not only as God, but at all?

At no time was any angel or apostle worshipped *except* when the worshipper mistook them as the source of the blessing rather than the channel. Nothing like this occurs in the male/female sexual dynamic. I do not worship my wife as the source of my blessings. I worship her as a channel of God's blessing and presence. I'm sure that if I told my wife that she was the Alpha and the Omega, she would revoke my worship license. I assure you that I have never asked my wife to atone for my sins, or to transform water into an alcoholic beverage.

And just who are women supposed to worship?

Good question. The answer is that they're not supposed to worship anyone; it's neither their bent nor their part of the parable. God has not wired women to worship men. I'm not saying that women are not passionate. They are passionate, but their passion leans toward receiving worship and adoration rather than giving it. It is only as they accept male worship and stop condemning men for it—and stop condemning themselves for their own "selfish" bent—that they become happy and fulfilled in marriage. In the worship department of God's marriage parable, one gender embodies the physical giving, and the other the physical receiving. It must be so. Gather a random handful of men and women and ask each if, in the realm of sex, they would rather give or receive worship. It is God Himself Who has thus wired the respective genders. Let us obey our natures. ***—MZ***

EXCERPTS

"Breathtaking. Beautiful. Inspired. I thank you from the bottom of my heart for making me feel my worth." *—Brenda O'Neil*

EXCERPT
Eve Raised

Women, as we have seen, are our better selves. It is our duty to keep them from struggle and harm. They are too precious to be exposed, challenged, shot at, stoned, tortured, shipwrecked, and raped. Why not spare the sons of Adam, that is, males? Because Adam was first molded, thereafter Eve. He is the expendable one; the one of whom we require this kind of sacrifice. The woman is his glory, and her we must preserve.

What nation sends its women to the front lines of wars? Any civilization worthy of the name protects its women and children from armed conflict for the same reason the Smithsonian protects the Hope Diamond. Is it that the Hope Diamond is not good enough to mingle with the other rocks? No. It's *too* good; it's *too* precious. It belongs to a more esteemed category than the other rocks.

The apostle Peter also wishes for women, "a meek and quiet spirit, which, in God's sight, is costly" (1 Peter 3:4).

Would that more women wished the same for themselves—and that more men wished to provide it. A quiet life is a promotion; it is an *upgrade* from teaching. It is more *costly* than teaching.

Even after the curse of Eden, men need women more than women need men.

Speaking of general mortality rates, by the age of 100, women outnumber men 8 to 1.

"And he shall rule over you." This mistranslation has wreaked immeasurable societal havoc. No wonder men lord it over women, and husbands over wives; they imagine that God, in Eden, decreed it. What a difference between "he shall rule over you" and "he shall rule *in* you," that is, in your heart. Rather than a warning to women and a command to men, this verse becomes a credit to women and a blessing to men. His welfare is now the burden of her heart. And his sexual clinging—"therefore a man will leave his father and his mother, and will cling into his woman" (Genesis 2:24, Dabhar Translation)—is the need of her heart. As if a man knows how to rule a woman anyway. Those who foolishly manage it employ intimidation and brute force, that is, violence. Superior strength is a man's only advantage over the fair sex.

Keep in mind that these things, as beneficial as they are (minus the sadness in childbearing), are things that *befell* Eve. They are consequences of sin. Whereas Adam was to cling to his woman from the moment of her creation (Genesis 2:21-24) *before* sin, her impulse and striving is not toward him or altogether receptive of him until after sin's entrance. Remember that 1 Corinthians 11:9—"Man is not created because of the woman, but the woman because of the man"—makes man the lacking one and woman his completion. True, God is the One Who made man to lack, but so be it. Before sin, Eve completed Adam by receiving his clinging. It is only after the entrance of sin that completion, for Adam, became part of Eve's need. She then *wanted* his clinging and sought his welfare. The physical pressing of her husband then became a springboard toward a previously unneeded marvel: emotional oneness.

Whenever I hear men gloating about being the heads of their homes and receiving more exceeding honor, I happily point out that God gives exceeding honor to that which is deficient. Pharaoh was deficient in every way to Joseph, yet still occupied the throne. "Congratulations on your exceeding honor," I say to the husbands. "This proves that you are deficient." It's true. The husbands walk away sulking. I always pray that they swallow their pride and learn how rewarding it is to serve the superior gender.

I continually marvel at God's paradoxes. God gives the lesser sex (males) the headship over the greater sex (females) because in God's odd way of doing business, the deficient (males) get more exceeding honor. And yet, the honor of the deficient (male) is to assume the Christ-like place and serve the more respectable member.

Why didn't God do it "the right way" in the first place and let women lead men without the power struggle? It's called exercise of character. God says: Let us see if man is wise enough to discern the proper direction for marriage (his headship), then bold enough to articulate it. Let us see if woman is humble enough to be taught, then bold enough to live the lesson. Let us see if the husband can trust his wife enough to acknowledge her house-managing wisdom, and the wife faithful enough (and, paradoxically, subject enough) to cherish that which has been entrusted to her.

No one can accuse God of doing things the easy way, yet who can match Him in the personal fulfillment department?

Men lack the covering afforded women; men are comparatively naked before God and Christ. Within the protection of Christ, we are the vulnerable ones, the expendable half. We see this both in political and spiritual warfare. God would have men die so that women might live. Never, in Scripture, is the converse true. This pictures Christ and His service to the ecclesia, or church.

Women are jewels, and men their temporary caretakers. We will never fully grasp either the elemental mystery of the diadem or its inherent worth. We can only marvel that such a prize is entrusted to us. May God inspire us to embrace this role for ourselves, for God, and for the glory of womanhood. ■

MARTIN ZENDER GOES TO HELL

"God used this small book to change my life.
After fifteen years in the pulpit, I finally
understand what hell is. Better late than never."
-J. Marcus Oglesby, M.Div.
MARTIN ZENDER
GOES TO HELL
MARTIN ZENDER
Author of "How to Quit Church Without Quitting God"

EXCERPT
Martin Zender Goes to Hell

When Adam sinned, what was the consequence? Go and see. Here was the worst sin ever. What better time to reveal the ultimate, horrible fate? But it's not there. You'll be driven from the Garden, Adam, and you'll have to hoe like mad to make anything grow. Eve, childbearing will introduce you to pain so severe you'll see white. And today, you begin to die, both of you. It's the penalty of your disobedience. Death and weeds and cramps the color of lightning. And I should mention this as well: I won't be coming around as often.

Bad enough, but not a word about an eternity of torture in flames. I wonder why. Do you?

Along comes Cain then, who murders his brother Abel. Murder is an unknown crime until then, but the worst since the Satan/Eve/fruit debacle. Now is a good time for God to unveil the Mother of All Punishments, to discourage future lawbreakers. But no, not a word about it. There is judgment, yes, but it's rational and reasonable: Cain's farming labors get cursed—the ground won't produce for him—and he has to wander the Earth as a nomad. We anticipate such phrases as, "Burn forever, murderer," or, "Go to hell, Cain," but they are not here.

I hope no one is disappointed.

What about in the days of Noah? The citizens of that era sinned as a profession. All people thought about back then was: How can we sin with more skill and greater efficiency? They loved their grim occupation and rarely took a break from it. If any people deserved eternal torment, it was these. Burn the blasphemers in hell forever? Surprisingly, no. The sinners merely got wiped out in a flood. Merely? Think about it. One glug and down came your curtain. It couldn't have been pleasant, but it was better than burning forever.

God does sometimes employ fire and brimstone to curtail the careers of professional sinners. Like Lysol, however, fire and brimstone kill germs on contact. (That is, the fire and brimstone do not eternally torment the germs.) Consider the twin cities of Sodom and Gomorrah, cities which today have become synonymous with sexual perversion. When the hour of reckoning arrived, "The Lord rained on Sodom and Gomorrah brimstone and fire from the Lord out of heaven" (Genesis 19:24). The result? God "destroyed the cities of the valley" (verse 29). Note the conspicuous absence of "God began to torment the inhabitants of these cities for eternity."

What about in the days of Moses, when there were laws for everything and a thousand ways to break them? Here's another ideal opportunity for the doctrine of eternal torment to begin "crawling all over Scripture," as I've been told that it is. And yet, it is another opportunity squandered by God and His servant Moses, who could get mad enough to smash rock. All threats in the days of Moses concerned earthly rewards and punishments only. Kill another man's bull, and your bull was killed. Mishandle some point of law, and your crops failed. Tangle with Moses himself, and some terrible thing happened with your wife's hormones. Or an enemy would storm your gates. Or both.

All bad enough, but not crazy. Nothing eternal and not a hint of unending flame. Capital punishment was by stoning then, the worst that could happen. It was nothing you wanted in on, but at least you died. One rock to the head relaxed you enough to dim the finish. No more taxes, tents, scorpions, sand storms, or Moses. For men and women toiling and failing upon an evil planet, death often came as a mercy.

To review, nowhere in the Old Testament does any God-inspired writer mention one word about an eternity of torment for disobeying God. Not one scholar has ever found it, no, not even those who have searched for it desperately. Strange that a doctrine that is "everywhere" has not yet appeared in a segment of the Bible that is, by my reckoning, about three and a half inches thick.

Is it that the amateurs of that delicate era could not shoulder such a responsibility? Then let the Old Testament lightweights stand aside to make way for Someone Who Knows How To Damn. Close the Old Testament books, and make way for genuine terror. Turn one page past Malachi, all ye sinners. To the Gospels! But rejoice not. Rather, fear. For you did not realize how good you had it in the days of old. You are about to pine for those days of flood, famine, and stone. For here, finally, comes One Rising to New Levels of Damnation, a Divine Unveiler of Heretofore Unimaginable Torture. His Good News, in a nutshell, is "Love Me before you die, or my Father will do worse than kill you!" His name? JESUS CHRIST, SAVIOR.

> The spirit of the Lord is on Me, on account of which He anoints Me to bring the evangel to the poor. He has commissioned Me to heal the crushed heart, to herald to captives a pardon, and to the blind the receiving of sight; to dispatch the oppressed with a pardon, to herald an acceptable year of the Lord...
>
> —*Jesus Christ, Luke 4:18-19*

Are you ready now to find out how things *really* are?

The most frightening threats Jesus made to the Israelites are probably those found in Matthew 5:29-30 and Mark 9:43-48. Here, Jesus explains how much better it is for an Israelite to pluck out his or her eye, or tear off his or her hand, than to let these members lead one into "the fire of hell." These verses have terrified countless millions over the centuries, people to whom the verses don't even apply. These are Israelite threats for an earthly, Israelite kingdom.

The "fire of hell"? That's bad translating. Jesus never said the word "hell" in His life. He didn't speak English. The word that left His lips was *Gehenna*. That's right. Jesus warned the Israelites about "the fire of Gehenna," not hell, and any concordance will confirm this for you (see word #1067 in Strong's, and page 474 in Young's.) Gehenna is a small valley along the southwest corner of Jerusalem. It's a geographical location, a place you can walk in today. God made sure that some versions of Scripture got this right (the *Concordant Literal New Testament*, *Rotherham's Emphasized Bible*, and *Young's Literal Translation*, to name three).

As any dictionary will tell you, Gehenna is where the Israelites of old dumped their garbage and offered sacrifices to foreign gods. In the old days it was called the Valley of Hinnom. From *The Random House Dictionary*, under the entry *Gehenna*: "The valley of Hinnom, near Jerusalem, where propitiatory sacrifices were made to Molech." It may be a pleasant green valley today, but in the 1,000-year kingdom it will function as a crematorium for the corpses of criminals (Isaiah 66:23-24).

The "fire of hell"? Here is the only instance where the *King James Version* has taken the name of an actual place and made it something else. Watch this: Where the Greek has *Hierousalem*, the KJV translates "Jerusalem"—every time. Where the Greek has *Nazaret*, the KJV makes it "Nazareth"—every time. Where the Greek has *Bethleem*, the KJV has "Bethlehem"—every time. This is sensible. It's an honorable and consistent way of translating. But here, where Jesus says *Gehenna* (another geographical location), the KJV (as well as the *New International Version*—NIV—and *New American Standard Bible*—NASB), makes it "hell." Gee, that's weird. Can you explain it? I can. Ever hear the phrase, "theological bias"?

Matthew, chapter 25. Here we find "the Son of Mankind come into His glory, seated on the throne." In front of Him are gathered "all the nations," and "He shall be severing them from one another even as a shepherd is severing the sheep from the goats." This judgment is advertised in your local church as "the final judgment" of "all humankind," when "God's enemies" go to either "heaven or hell," for "all eternity." But no. Each sheep and goat represents a nation, not a person. This is not Uncle Harry standing before Jesus; it is Ethiopia. It is not Aunt Hazel trembling before Him; it is Russia. It is not Jim the milkman; it is Afghanistan.

This judgment occurs at the inauguration of the thousand-year kingdom, in the valley of Jehoshaphat. Like Gehenna, this is a literal, geographical location outside Jerusalem (see map again on page 37). As with Gehenna's fire and worms, this judgment is practical. Jesus returns to find Earth's political alignments amok. Good nations will be low; the evil will sit on high. The Great Judge will cure this. What criteria will He use for judging? Their belief in Him? Their confession of faith? The mode of their baptism? No. It will be that nation's policy toward Israel, nothing more. No one will ask, "What church did you go to?" or, "Why didn't you have more faith?"

To make this the general judgment of all humanity is to slaughter the context. But who cares? The possibility of a near-universal twisting of this judgment, and a vast misrepresentation of God's character, will not bother most people. Why? I will tell you. ■

Dear Martin,
I have just finished *Martin Zender Goes to Hell*. This is one of the best books I have ever read. All anxiety over my loved ones has vanished. Praise God! The facts you present are unassailable. —*Stephen S.*

EXCERPT
FLAWED BY DESIGN

A woman crashes into the home of Simon the Pharisee. The town sinner, she neither knocks nor removes her sandals. Whoredom is fresh on her clothes, yet something belying this rests angelically upon her face. Only one person here can appreciate the transformation. The woman hurries to the feet of the Master.

An unusual thing had occurred in the early morning hours of that day, after the last man (the last client) had slipped into the Jerusalem night. As she looked about her cubicle, a dread of the future gripped her. Why should she feel this now? Why tonight? No immediate answer came, yet a vision of her final hours flickered in the flame of her one remaining candle. She would die in this room; which night, she did not know. It would be soon, though. Death would come slowly in a pool of blood, released onto the floor by her own hand. Her sister Mariba would find her. Mariba would scream, there would be a funeral—thirty days of mourning—then it would all be over.

The walls closed in. Stars twinkled outside these walls, somewhere. A sun shone on the other side of Earth, though not for her. For her there was only the shadow cast by her burning piece of wax, a leather-like ghost running from her feet to a corner, up a wall, across the ceiling, then back to her naked feet. Nothing could escape the cubicle. Floor, wall, ceiling, then back to engulf her. Her hands went to her face now; she was crying.

She had to get out.

Not one other soul occupied the side street where she burst from her home. Urgency along this void of humanity became her silent scream. She would not break down in the city.

Outside the Essene gate, down the valley of Hinnom, up over the aqueduct, then west toward the Bethlehem Road; this brought her to the field. Recently gleaned, dead and quiet, the soil sent coolness into her legs. From above, the heavens lay frozen and mute. Between these two voids she fell to her knees to gather a piece of Earth. Instead, she found a stone, for God had placed it there centuries ago, for her to find. Now it would become her means of hating Him. She picked up the stone as a man would grasp it, then found her feet. Her left eye was already trained into the heavens, right wrist cocked toward the throne room.

All agonies now shifted to the act of throwing. Every sinew, muscle, joint, and fragment of despair made ready the rock for the face of God. She would hit Him, yes. And her tongue, too, lay poised with the forbidden question, "What have You *made* me?!"

The stone traveled a little way into space, propelled by the impetus of the word "made." But then it returned to Earth, though she never heard where.

She had missed.

The forbidden question, however, had not missed at all. In fact, it had hit squarely, and she knew it. Something had happened. Now she felt millions of invisible eyes. She had unmistakably commanded something, perhaps everything. The field was now a stage. With knowledge of this came a liberating rush of boldness. What happened next happened too quickly to stop.

Frustrated with your failures? Feeling condemned? Can't overcome a bad habit? I've got great news for you:

"Now we have this treasure in earthen vessels, that the transcendence of the power may be of God and not of us" (2 Corinthians 4:7).

Your humble little vessel of sin is made that way on purpose. We are clay pots by design, not because we have gone afoul of God's intention for us. Let this revelation soothe the exhausted self-improver. Retire, Christian soldier! You fail by design, not because you are a failure. God wants you cognizant of the source of your power, and He has many creative ways of driving this home. One of these is sin.

Wouldn't some of us love to shed our earthenware now and still walk among mortals? Our sins keep us from producing a perfect walk, and we mourn this. What we do not understand is that an imperfect walk is the main idea of this life. God puts the treasure of His spirit in earthen vessels now to keep the vessels from situating themselves upon high places. A perfect walk is not what we need right now. Who could live with us? Could we stand ourselves? Humility is a blessed thing this side of resurrection. Vessels on high shelves sit poised, ready to topple and shatter upon hard floors. Pride is burdensome and is known for preceding falls. Can it be so bad to be delivered of this?

Thank God for the comfort of mistakes. Mistakes remind us of our clayhood and drive us toward Christ. When we finally quit chasing perfection and accept these vessels of clay, we will become happier. When we forget about ourselves, peace will ensue. The happy acceptance of imperfection is the beginning of easy breathing. Because, really, how can you be peaceful and flogging yourself simultaneously? You can't. That's why no one in a religion is truly happy. People in religions act happy because they're expected to, but they're only one step away from disappointing their deity and suffering his wrath. How happy can they truly be?

In the Bible, God is always getting humans into scrapes so that He can get them out of the scrapes and show His power. You say, "No, Martin. God isn't getting the humans into the scrapes. The humans are getting themselves into the scrapes." Well, that theory works fine until you consider accounts such as the hardening of Pharaoh's heart. And we're going to do that shortly. But first I want to show you how God delights in making things humanly impossible before He sets to work.

Remember the story of the blind man Christ healed? What is the first thing the Lord does? He spits on the ground, makes mud, and then smears the mud on the man's eyes. Then He tells the man to go wash in the Pool of Siloam. The guy comes back reading *The Jerusalem Post.* Just when you think God is crazy with this mud business, you start to wonder, *Maybe God is making a point. Maybe mud on top of blindness is God's way of compounding a problem.*

Consider 1 Kings, chapter 18, when Elijah challenged the prophets of the false god Baal to a contest, to see which God was real. Elijah and the prophets of Baal would each set up an altar. Each would pray to their God to send fire down to their respective altars. The God who sent fire down would be the true God. The prophets of Baal went first.

According to verse 26 of that chapter, the prophets of Baal "called on the name of Baal from morning until noon, saying, 'O Baal, answer us.' But there was no voice and no one answered. And they leaped about the altar which they made."

No Baal. It was Elijah's turn.

Notice the curious thing Elijah does to his altar. I'm quoting from verses 33-35. Elijah said, "'Fill four pitchers with water and pour it on the burnt offering and on the wood.' And he said, 'Do it a second time,' and they did it a second time. And he said, 'Do it a third time,' and they did it a third time. And the water flowed around the altar, and he also filled the trench with water.'"

With the dousing of the altar, Elijah, through the spirit of God, was setting up a field of "impossibility" on which God would demonstrate His power.

Is God making some things impossible for you? Is God dousing your life with water? And when you seem about to recover, is He dousing you a second time? Then a third time? Is there running water in the trenches of your life? Are you getting ready to put on your swimsuit, sit down, and stare at your insurmountable trials? Good. The sooner you do that, the better off you'll be. God has purposely dampened your life with impossibilities, in order to bring you to the end of yourself. The result is that you will be in a relaxed position (flat on your back, for instance, or on your face) to hear and see His new plan for your life. ■

Martin,

I heard you on a radio show in Chattanooga, TN about a year ago. You debated a Baptist minister. The host sent me one of your books: *Flawed by Design*. I had been a Baptist from a young age until about twenty. Then there were too many questions that didn't add up, so I became mostly an atheist.

When I read your book, I nearly went deaf because of all the clicking sounds. Those were the sounds of all those things in the Bible that didn't add up, clicking into place. I credit your book as the means God used to allow faith in Him to return to me. I now realize that Christ died on the cross for all our sins and His grace is sufficient to save us. —*John P.*

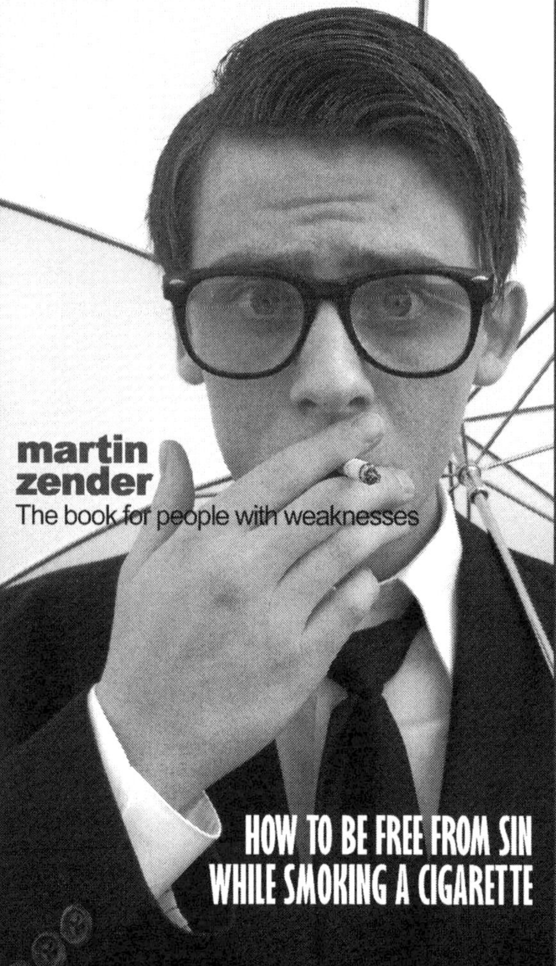
martin
zender
The book for people with weaknesses
HOW TO BE FREE FROM SIN
WHILE SMOKING A CIGARETTE

EXCERPT

How to be Free From Sin While Smoking a Cigarette

I don't smoke, but I sometimes wish I did. I have other questionable habits I won't burden you with. But I can picture myself holding a cigarette, or letting it hang cockeyed out of my mouth like Humphrey Bogart used to do. Whenever I talked—mumbled, I mean—the cigarette would bounce up and down. Then I'd squint and say something devilish to Lauren Bacall.

In this fantasy of mine, I know smoking is bad for me. I know it's wrong. I know I'm sinning, even while I'm doing it. But I do it anyway because it's cool, because life has been unfair to me, because Bacall has great legs, and because if I don't do *something*, I'll lose my mind. It's the worse kind of sin: knowing it's bad, but doing it anyway.

Preachers today lower their voices when speaking of such badness. They'll talk all sing-songy about stock sins like anger, jealousy, and pride. I call these stock sins because they're a dime a dozen. I'm not saying they're not bad, but I find myself doing them without even thinking. The sins I'm talking about—the sins that make the preachers furrow their eyebrows and talk like Vincent Price—are the ones where the wretched sinner says, "Yes, this would be a sin, all right," then does it anyway.

According to the clergy, there's no refuge for this. It's not like it's an accidental sin. It's not like it's a one-time deal. It's more like, "We're sorry, Lord, for what we did today. And we're sorry, too, that we're probably going to do it again tomorrow. And the day after that. And the day after that." The only comfort from the pulpit for this kind of badness is the remote possibility of a Sno-cone stand in hell. So no matter what your particular weakness is—

Well, hold on a minute. It just occurred to me that maybe you don't have a weakness. This is something I had not considered until now, and it changes everything. This project is shot if most of my readers don't have a weakness. If you don't have a weakness, how can I let you waste your time reading a book about weaknesses and how to deal with them? If you don't have a weakness, then please accept my apology, return this book to your bookseller, and use the money you saved to send a real sinner to Bible camp.

This book is written only for those who know what they're supposed to do but sometimes don't do it. It's written for those who think that their own particular weakness keeps God from completely liking them. It's written for those who just can't shake a bad habit. This book is written for the wretched souls who totter between their passion life and their desire for God, not realizing that in order to have a desire for God they must also be dogged by at least one nagging passion that keeps them humble and needing Him. It was wrong of me to assume the worst of you. So forgive me, please, and have a blessed day.

For those who do have a weakness—or two—welcome to paragraph seven. It appears that we've lost a few of the religious folks. At least now we can speak honestly among ourselves.

We're believers. Or we're seekers. Some of us love Jesus Christ already; others aren't sure if we want to or not. In either case, there are bad things we all do occasionally (or continually, perhaps) that dismantle our happiness in front of God. They've got a term for this dismantling that is so weighty and terrible it deserves its own paragraph.

The term is guilt.

Is it possible to be free from sin, even while sinning? Is it possible to be free from sin and the guilt associated with it, even while narrowing your eyes at Bacall and leaning toward her match?

I know what religion has told you. Religion has told you that freedom from sin means you don't sin anymore. But is this God's thought? If this is God's thought, then no one today can be free from sin—at least none of the honest people who made it past paragraph six. But I generally find that God's thoughts and the thoughts of orthodox religion are two different things. I'm happy to report it's also the case here.

This book is written and dedicated to all the poor sinners in the world who can't stop sinning, but who love or want to love the Lord, Jesus Christ. Here's the good news: *You have already been freed from sin.*

Thanks for hanging on. God's Word is about to deliver you from discouragement, condemnation and guilt, without asking you to change a thing you're doing. On second thought, you may have to change one thing. If you've been beating yourself over the head trying not to sin, you're going to have to quit that. Stop assaulting your head.

You still here? Great. That last paragraph wasn't a joke. I would never joke about something as serious as sin. How could I possibly tell you to quit pummeling yourself over it? Because this monumental effort—and the repeated failures and inevitable guilt trips that follow—is ruining your opinion of yourself, taking away your peace, and robbing you of the affection due Christ. You're working so hard trying to *impress* Him that you're not paying enough attention *to* Him.

"But if I let down my guard for even a second," you say, "I'll sin like a crazy person."

Hold on. That's what religion has told you, and I just suggested that religion is usually wrong. It's wrong here, for sure. Religion supposes that by keeping a moral watchdog chained to your flesh, you'll stop sinning. You've probably already disproved this theory with many a botched New Year's resolution. The Pharisees disproved it 2,000 years ago.

Before his trial, Scripture describes Job as "flawless and upright." This is verse 1 of chapter 1. But then Job loses his family, his wealth, and his health. Now listen to him in chapter 10, verse 1: "My soul is disgusted with my life; let me give free rein to myself and my concern; let me speak in the bitterness of my soul." Ah, there's the real Job, the mess of a man that was seething beneath that skin all along. But before he could understand his weakness, Job had to be broken. Can you imagine your Christian brother or sister even thinking Job's "blasphemous" words? No one would invite the real Job to the Wednesday prayer meeting, at least not without asking him to comb his hair and keep his scabby mouth shut.

George Bernard Shaw was a genius. It was he who said: "Virtue is insufficient temptation." Many times, those who appear virtuous have not been sufficiently tempted. Their virtue is Hollywood-wall virtue, propped up with half a dozen two-by-fours and a New Year's resolution. It's self-control untested. The world can spot phony Christian virtue ten miles away. Christians can't see it because they are too busy admiring themselves in the mirror.

Real human virtue is being broken by trial and lying like a pile of lumber in the wake of a hurricane. That's when the good stuff starts; it's when God goes to work. Real human virtue is helplessness before God. Helplessness before God is the beginning of a true spirituality that stands strong when the wind blows. Well, it has no place to go but up.

Romans 5:8—"Yet God is commending this love of His to us, seeing that, while we are still sinners, Christ died for our sakes."

God went out of His way here to say, in effect, "I did not justify you in your Sunday clothes. I did not justify you while you were loving your neighbor as yourself, or praying to Me in the quietness of your room. Instead, I justified you while you were yelling at your children, running up your credit card, stuffing yourself with donuts—and worse. I did this for you on your worst day, not your best. I did it this way so that you could thank Me the rest of your life instead of wasting your time trying to figure out how to downplay your faults and impress Me."

What did you say, God? Our robes were rustling.

When God justifies us this way, we're finished before we start. Since He did His best for us at our worst, what can we do now to improve the relationship? Act better? But He already did His best for us while we were acting our worst. What can we do now to blow our relationship with Him? Sin? But He already maxed out on His love for us while we were sinning like crazy people. ■

Dear Martin,

I stumbled across your book at the library while researching other faiths and was instantly intrigued. As I read, I could literally feel the guilt falling off of me. I swear I feel 10 pounds lighter each day because I no longer pack my sins around with me. I feel the love of God more clearly now than ever. The reality of God's grace is beautiful. The pure logic of it is so obvious now, but was so hidden before. Thanks be to Him, and to you for voicing it. The only regret I have is that it took so long for me to truly experience the power of the cross. *—Susan R.*

Beyond Politics
What to do while we're here

martin
zender

EXCERPT
BEYOND POLITICS

According to the apostle Paul in 2 Timothy, in the last days perilous periods will be present and nothing is going to stop them, not even Republicans. Anyone supposing that in the last days humanity will perfect itself is thinking his or her own pleasant thoughts and is out of tune with the mind of God. Our Lord Jesus Christ is not returning to Earth to congratulate us on a job well done. He is coming to sweep away the perilous periods and establish something that we have never seen before: righteous government. And so—

"Cease striving and know that I am God…I will be exalted in the earth" (Psalm 46:10).

"God's indignation is being revealed from heaven on all the irreverence and injustice of humans" (Romans 1:18).

God has promised to take care of the irreverent and unjust, but He will do it in His time, not in ours. Jesus chided Peter for taking up the sword in Gethsemane, saying, "Are you supposing that I am not able to entreat My Father, and at present He will station by My side more than twelve legions of messengers? How, then, may the scriptures be fulfilled, seeing that thus it must occur?" (Matthew 26:53-54). It's the same situation today.

Few understand today that God is able, at any time, to reveal His indignation on irreverence and injustice. I have to remind myself of this all the time. The fact that He has not yet moved to impress upon Earth's inhabitants His power means only one thing: it's not yet time for it. When the hour does arrive, God will turn the sun black, make the stars fall, roll up the heavens, move islands, burn up thirty-three percent of the earth, and turn a third of the sea into blood (Revelation 6:12-14, 8:7-8).

I guess that will be impressive enough.

Not only is it wrong to worry about the moral downslide of America and its leaders (Philippians 4:6), but no slave of the Lord will be found fighting it (2 Timothy 2:24). A decline must take place (2 Timothy 3:1-9, Daniel 12:9-10), and happy is the soul taking refuge in God until destruction passes by (Psalm 57:1). Concerning those vessels of dishonor destined to carry out the end-time decadence (Romans 9:21-23, Proverbs 16:4, Revelation 22:11), Paul's advice to believers is to shun them (2 Timothy 3:6), not fight or reform them. It is not ours to be judging those who are outside. "Now those outside, God is judging" (1 Corinthians 5:13).

God is the One Who is operating all in accord with the counsel of His will (Ephesians 1:11). For those of you who do want to cease striving but have been intimidated out of it by your politically active Christian friends, may this book provide your long-sought Scriptural grounds for minding things above (the heavenly kingdom), not things on earth.

Concerning national defense, I am not so pie-in-the-sky that I think we should write national policy based on trust. I wish that we could, but the eon in which we live is naughty, not nice. It's a wicked eon (Galatians 1:4), and thus it is naïve for us to think that we can sit down and negotiate with sinister entities. Neville Chamberlain tried that with Hitler, and it did not end so well. We ended up ditching Chamberlain and bombing the crap out of Hitler. In a wicked eon, we need a strong military. I am proud of our soldiers, and thankful for them.

I'm speaking of national policy now, and not the policy of individuals. I am not personally going to chase down evil dictators; I'm afraid I would catch them. But I think it's good for our armed forces to do so; they *want* to catch them, and should. We must protect our homeland. If an evil dictator entered my literal house and threatened my family, I would stab him repeatedly with a screwdriver. (I don't own a gun. I'm all for gun-owning, I just don't like loud noises.)

An evil dictator striding through my kitchen is a microcosm of an army entering our fair land. It is a natural instinct to protect loved ones as long as it's not too noisy. And yet an individual believer may choose the path of non-resistance, which is the most excellent path. I'll be talking about that later—about whether or not we should be subject to evil governments.

People tell me that I have to know what's going on in the world. I say, "show me the verse." It's fascinating, but no one has yet shown me the verse. If there were such a verse, I am convinced that I would have been shown it by now. I have not taken a newspaper, ever. People have said to me, "Why don't you get the paper, Zender?" and my stock answer is, "Because I might find out what's happening in the world." I don't understand how people can read newspapers and live to tell about it. Well, they generally don't live. They get cancer and die. It takes a little time to die of worry, but it happens eventually.

Reading newspapers is the very definition of minding things of the earth. It's like going to a restaurant and saying, "Give me your War Special and a side order of Worry. For dessert, I would like a large Plane Crash and a Communist Coup." Good God. What do you expect? How can you expect peace when you order an entrée of War? I am not even mentioning the 11:00 news, but don't get me started. Oh, it's too late. "Honey. Turn on the news. Let's watch colorful, hi-definition accounts of kidnappings, rapes, racial discord, house fires, and tsunamis in faraway places. Then we'll go nite-nite." ■

HOW TO QUIT CHURCH
WITHOUT QUITTING GOD

"A provocative, intellectual romp. You need to read this book!"
--Dwight Green
Ft. Worth Star-Telegram

martin zender

HOW TO QUIT CHURCH WITHOUT QUITTING GOD

Why going to church today is unbiblical, un-Christlike, and spiritually risky.

How to Quit Church Without Quitting God

"Confronting hypocrisy, contradiction, and cult overtones in modern-day Christianity head-on, Zender raises serious criticisms without renouncing true faith. A truly fascinating book, and compelling reading for faithful churchgoers and disillusioned church members alike."

Michael J. Carson
The Midwest Book Review

"Zender's book will no doubt cause great irritation to clergy members everywhere. But it's only because no one has had the courage to state ideas as critical as his."

Dan Julian
The State News

"Zender's conversational writing style turns discussion about strict religious dogma into a fun-filled frolic. Although vehemently spiritual, he is the Robin Williams of the roadside tent revival. It is a provocative, intellectual romp through the Bible basics."

Dwight Greene
Fort Worth Star-Telegram

"Zender writes in such an informed, entertaining, and challenging way that one experiences a whole series of epiphanies as they make their way through this delightful look at how religion works in our lives."

Alan Caruba
Bookviews

"Reading Zender makes you laugh, gets you mad, and starts you to thinking. His snappy, in-your-face writing grabs you as he forcefully tackles hypocrisy that masquerades as religion."

Chris Meehan
The Kalamazoo Gazette

"An excellent book that is part of what are probably the three best books on the problems of the church today."

Harold McFarland
Readers Preference Reviews

EXCERPT
How To Quit Church Without Quitting God

This book describes the joy and freedom you will experience by quitting organized religion. By necessity, it must expose the world's most popular religion, and the hypocrisies that poison it. The way I see it, no one can properly enjoy God from the perspective of an institution. But who will quit the institution if they think that everything is "just fine" there? But nothing is "just fine" there, not even close. So I sound the call to freedom. I do this, not by promoting my own authority or instructing you from my podium (the method of most "how-to" authors), but by pointing out the spiders on the institution walls and demonstrating how green (and pest-free) is the grass on the other side.

I believe one of the main reasons the world rejects Jesus Christ is that it thinks He's a member of the religion bearing His name. If only the world realized how much Jesus hates hypocrisy, ice-cream socials and repetitive worship songs, they would depart without compunction. I saw a bumper sticker recently that said, "I have no problem with God, it's His fan club I can't stand."

Millions of church people today secretly want to quit church, but they balk because they think that if they quit church, they'll be quitting God. No. God and His Son quit organized religion years ago, and haven't been back. (Well, they never were members in the first place.) And would you believe me if I told you that not one person in the Bible ever "went to church"? The church is a people, not an address on Main Street. One does not *go* to it, one *is* it.

Do you go to church every week? Then this book will challenge you. Have you walked away from organized religion? Then this book will comfort you. Have you avoided religion all your life?

You may be a spiritual genius. ■

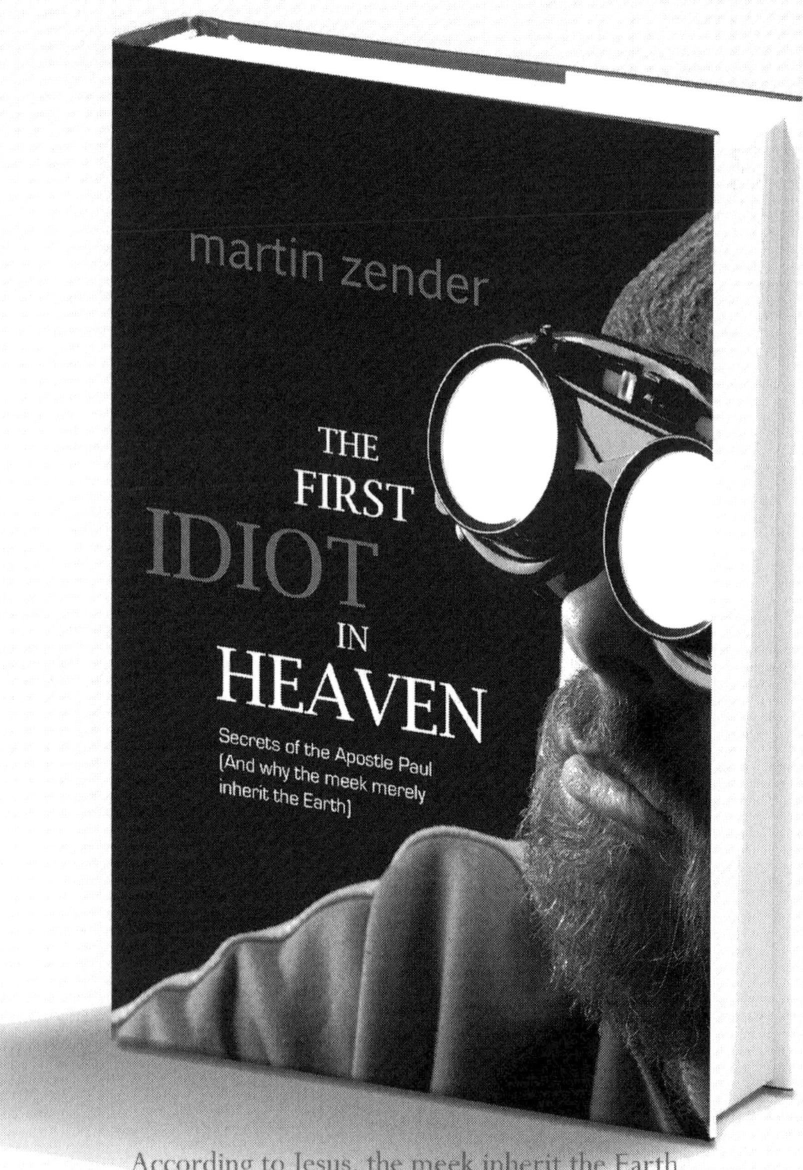
martin zender
THE FIRST IDIOT IN HEAVEN
Secrets of the Apostle Paul (And why the meek merely inherit the Earth)

EXCERPT

The First Idiot In Heaven

While on Earth, Jesus said some difficult things. He told the rich to give away all their money, and the joyful to become mourners. If you wanted to inherit the Earth, you had to be meek. If your eye offended you, no problem—as long as you plucked it out. A friend of mine said, "Can I start following Jesus on Monday? I'd like to enjoy the weekend."

The words and commandments of Jesus are pure, perfect, holy—and meant for Israelites. Jesus Himself said, "I was not sent except to the lost sheep of the house of Israel" (Matthew 15:24).

Is it possible that we have been struggling along someone else's path? What if the words in red were never meant to be our marching orders?

Several months after leaving Earth, the Jewish Messiah appeared as a very non-Jewish light to a self-righteous idiot en route to Damascus to kill Christians.

Up next? Not only a startling new destiny for believers (heaven instead of Earth) but a new message of pure grace for all humanity.

This is that story.

You want to live like Jesus, you really do. You're sincere as can be, but it's an uphill climb. You love people and you love God, so maybe today will be the day you can finally imitate His Son. Maybe today you can finally be meek, turn the other cheek, and rejoice while getting mud thrown in your face.

Think how good it would feel to be pure—to have no sin and no guilt. Think how good it would feel to wake up calm each morning, love everyone during the day, and rest your head at night with a prayer for your enemies.

If only.

And yet it never quite works out that way. In the darkness of your bed each night, you know who you are. Jesus was Jesus, but you are you. When you curl up beneath the covers, you face the terrible truth: It has been another day of failure and frustration.

If only there were a gospel in the Bible for common, ordinary human beings. Or even mediocre people. It seems the gospel of Jesus that tells us to live like Jesus sets the bar just a little too, um, *high.*

I know all about it. I was raised Catholic. The nuns told me that all I had to do was be meek and mild like Jesus (plus do everything else like Jesus) and I would go to heaven. It seemed like a tall order for a kid who still had cartoon characters on his underpants. What did I know? All I wanted was to play football and eat candy.

Why do we have such a difficult time shaping up and producing fruit worthy of repentance? Maybe better to ask: Why do we instinctively know we *can't* do these things? Why do we give up *trying* to do them? Is it because we are lazy? Ungodly? Satanic? Because we think we deserve nothing more than to be crushed beneath God's fist? Or could it be that, deep down, we think God doesn't really expect us to weep and wail, repent, and be practically perfect in every way? But if He doesn't expect all that, what do we do with all the Bible verses saying He does expect it? Could it be that there are *other* Bible verses that say *different* things?

Are you bold enough to entertain a new thought? What if we, who are not Israelites, have a different gospel—*in the Bible*—than the one meant for Israel? What if this other gospel even has a different name? What if it has a different set of requirements (and a different outlook on run-of-the-mill people or hapless nincompoops) than the gospel given to Israel? And—think of this—what if this gospel promises an enormously better destiny than the one promised to Jewish believers?

Were faithful Israelites ever promised heaven? Not once. Jesus Himself said, "The meek shall inherit *the earth*" (Matthew 5:5). Wouldn't Jesus have known what He was talking about? Israelites never dreamed of getting lifted from Terra Firma. Why would they? Jesus never spoke to them of such a thing. And neither did their prophets. Faithful Israelites were promised that they would rule and reign over the other nations of Earth. This was the promise God made to Abraham.

Back to my question. What if this different gospel I have been referring to (the easier one; the kinder and gentler one; the one that caters to those of us who are not-so-perfect) *does* take people to heaven? Wouldn't that be mind-boggling? It would mean that the nuns at my school were all wrong. Imitating the walk of Jesus would not have gotten me to heaven—as they insisted it would—but would, instead, have kept me on Earth to rule the other nations. What *would* get me to heaven would be giving up trying to be like Jesus and embracing a gospel for regular folks—assuming such a gospel actually exists.

Wouldn't that be something God would do? Bless the socks off average, ordinary people? Doesn't it align with everything we know about His penchant to stun loser-types (fishermen, prostitutes, tax-collectors) with draughts of favor? So God gives reformed sinners (obedient Israelites) what He promised them—namely, Earth—but then later announces a *different* gospel that seats unworthy people (those who haven't a prayer of being like His Son) at His right hand in the highest regions of heaven.

Would this be a gospel you'd like to learn about? ■

MORE READER COMMENTS:
The First Idiot in Heaven

"Martin, What can I say? Wow! Thank-you. I just ordered a bunch of *First Idiots* to give to friends who love wisdom, humor, and revelation. Everything was laid out just right, and succinct. Paul himself would be amazed. Thank you for not giving up your calling." —Kathy K.

"Hi Martin. I'm having a book while reading your beer! It's very, very good, but you've gotta know: They're gonna kill you for this one Zender ;) Love your work! Grace and peace from Norway!" —Erik S.

"I have been a Zender fan since his first book took the scum off of my eyes 15 years ago and gave me great peace. This book is a continuation of that peace. I can only say: Thanks, Martin. Were it not for you and your books, I would be truly confoused and lost in a man-made religion." —Bud M.

"Wow! Just finished *The First Idiot in Heaven*, and I think it is your best book yet. That's a big deal, since the others were so excellent. I hated to see the pages count down to 0." —James F.

"A must-read. The Evangel entrusted to Paul is so beautiful when contrasted with the Circumcision gospel. This book clearly differentiates the two. My prayer is that Father opens many hearts to *The First Idiot in Heaven.* This is a classic Zender book to be read and reread." —Max P.

"Best Zender book ever! (That's saying a lot.) I love the delivery, the humor, the wisdom. From the moment I picked up this book, I only put it down to go to work. Instant classic." —Darron H.

"Written with such clarity. Liberating, and nearly effortless to understand. No more anguish, guilt, shame. Martin, THANK YOU." —Susan L.

"This is the methodical, Scripturally-backed work I've always longed for. My deepest questions are answered. An articulate illustration of the difference between the writings of Paul and the rest of the Bible. Clearly, Martin's most powerful book to date." —Jana L.

All my life, since I was about 6, I knew God was not in a box, knew there was freedom. In February of 2009, I heard you and Dan on the radio for the first time. My kids and their friends have always known me to be someone who stuck with God's word and Holy Spirit, rather than with some slick preacher or formal church. I literally cried when I heard you guys for the first time! I wonder if you really realize how dramatic this can be for folks who feel like they have just come home? Thank you for being bold!

—*C.V., San Francisco*

My husband, 2 grown sons and I have been listening to your daily messages for a couple of years now. You are refreshingly different. I've been on a search for truth for about 10 years. We listened to a variety of Internet messages but settled on yours because it's dependable, funny, and best of all is NOT like regular church teaching. The gift you've been given is clarity. It's not a commonly possessed gift! *—M.R., Atlanta*

Dear Martin, Please keep the Clanging Gong News coming! We are a couple of families living in eastern Iowa, and have been getting together for fellowship for a few years now. Yo are a breath of fresh air to us! I have been known to read sections of your newsletter out loud, with tears in my eyes. God put you in our lives at exactly the right time. Keep doing what you do! *—A. B., Cedar Rapids*

Volume 1, Issue 21
July 4, 2009

Martin Zender's
Clanging Gong News
"If I know all mysteries and all knowledge, but have no love, I am a clanging gong" --1 Cor. 13:1-2

Two out of three isn't bad.

God is a man. Not.

From last week's mailbag:

Dear Martin: So what you're saying is that all the misery and pain in the world, God is responsible for. That seems very twisted and punitive to me, like we have this capricious God playing a cosmic chess game. I can't say I like serving a God like that.

—B.T. Memphis, TN

Dear B.T.

If you're serving a God like that, then you're serving a God of your own invention. God is neither twisted, punitive, nor capricious. And he does not play games.

I'm sure this chess player is a nice man. But he isn't God.

Concerning misery and pain, it's not about what I'm saying, but about what Ephesians 1:11 is saying: "God operates all in accord with the counsel of His will." So yes, "all" would certainly include all misery and pain. Your job is to believe Ephesians 1:11 and then trust God. Instead, you're believing Ephesians 1:11, but then assuming that God is a man; man is twisted, punitive, capricious, and a game player. Yikes, B.T. Are you sure you want to put the Deity into that same category?

The vital point of last week's edition was: temporary evil is essential to eternal bliss. The vital point here is: God is not a man.

Yours because of grace,

Martin

Behind the scenes at the creation of Satan

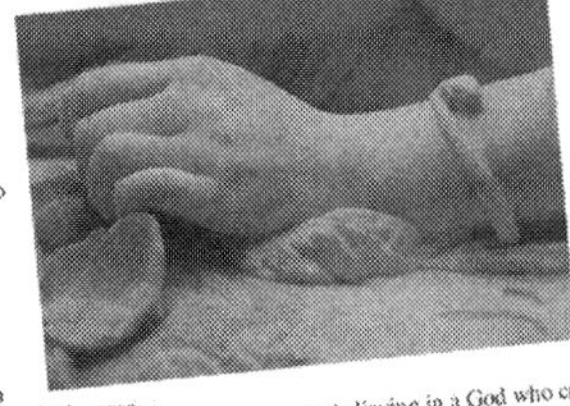

Before He could demonstrate His power, love, and salvation, God needed an enemy to wrestle against. Since enemies were once non-existent, God had to create His own. God did not enjoy creating an adversary. In fact, He hated it; it pained His heart. And yet, for the ultimate sake of His creatures, He had to do it. So He did.

I pray that, by the time you finish this article, you will see God's heart in the creation of evil. I want you to see how hard it was for Him (in the short term) to provide for your eternal happiness and security. As I have discussed with you before, there can be no such thing as eternal happiness and eternal security without the very real and painful struggle against adversity. God did this for you, not to you. Still, He wrestled with it.

You believe Him, but you hesitate to embrace Him.

Some of you are writing me—especially on the heels of last week's edition—telling me how you balk against believing in a God who created evil (Isaiah 45:7), and made the Adversary the way he is (Jn. 8:44; 1 Jn. 3:8). Those of you strong enough to accept this scriptural fact tend to hold such a God at arm's length. It's as if you do not fully trust Him. You can *believe* in a God Who creates evil, but you hesitate to embrace that One. Deep down, you fear Him. Today, I want you to change your heart and mind about God.

How can you continue fearing your Father? How can you continue fearing the One Who demonstrated His love for you by sending His only Son to die for your sake? How can you

(Continued on page 2)

ALL THE TRUTH THAT'S FIT TO PRINT.

85 free issues of Martin Zender's

Clanging Gong News

only at www.martinzender.com

YouTube